WITCH WAY'S
BOOK OF
100
LOVE SPELLS

EDITED BY
TONYA A. BROWN

First Edition, 2021

Tonya A. Brown
3436 Magazine St
#460
New Orleans, LA 70115
www.witchwaypublishing.com

Copyright © 2021 by Tonya A. Brown

Editor: Tonya A. Brown
Assistant Editor: Paul Flagg
Cover Designer: Olivie Blake
Illustrators: Stefanie Pillert and Adrian Delp
Internal Design: Emily Barta and Tonya A. Brown

All rights reserved. This book or any portion thereof may not be reproduced or used in any manner whatsoever without the express written permission of the publisher except for the use of brief quotations in a book review.

Printed in the United States of America

ISBN 978-1-087-8860-53

Dedicated to those who have not had an easy journey in love. For those who have experienced traumas that have led to fear or self-hatred. Those who believe they are not worthy of love or those who love the unattainable.

You are not alone.

CONTENTS

FOREWORD **XIII** Michael Herkes

INTRODUCTION **XV** Tonya A. Brown

PART I
RITUAL SPELLS

1

FREE WILL AND ETHICS	2	Michelle Guerrero Denison
ATTRACT COMMITMENT	9	Rebecca Ferreira Troy
GLAMOUR WITH SIGHT	10	Michael Herkes
CONJURE LOVE	11	Rebecca Ferreira Troy
HOW TO BOND WITH A SPIRIT LOVER AND FAMILIAR	12	Effy Winter
NEW RELATIONSHIP COMMUNICATION	13	Kiki Dombrowski
TRUE LOVE SPELL	15	Jessica Ripley
ENHANCE YOUR GLAM	16	Michael Herkes
COME TO ME	19	Michael Herkes
EXPLORE LOVE INCANTATIONS	20	Kiki Dombrowski

CONTENTS

STRENGTHEN NON-ROMANTIC LOVE	21	Nessa Skinner
ROSE RITUAL	23	Scarlet Ravenswood
AMAS VERITAS	24	Em Miiller
RELATIONSHIP STRENGTH	26	Michael Herkes
SELF-CARE RITUAL	27	Jenny Parten
SACRIFICE YOUR BROKEN HEART	28	Michael Herkes
FULL MOON SOULMATE RITUAL	31	Daina Renton
TURN FEAR INTO LOVE	32	Emme Dice
HOODOO CANDLE MAGIC FOR ATTRACTING A LOVER	33	Hoodoo Goddess
GET NOTICED	34	Michael Herkes
BRING LOVE TALISMAN	35	Rebecca Ferreira Troy
MAGIC THROUGH TOUCH	36	Michael Herkes
LOVE DRAWING RITUAL BATH	38	Emma Kathryn
MAGIC MIRROR LOVE SPELL	39	Kiki Dombrowski
A LOVE SPELL: INSPIRED BY THE LOVE WITCH	40	Michael Herkes
NEW MOON SELF-LOVE	43	Michael Herkes

CONTENTS

PART II
HERBAL / CRYSTAL SPELLS
☽ 45 ☾

INTRODUCTION	46	Michael Herkes
CINNAMON FOR LUST	51	Natalie J. Wilson
PASSIONFLOWER IN LOVE MAGIC	52	Kiki Dombrowski
CARDAMOM FOR LOVE	53	Jessica Ripley
LOVE SPELL JAR	54	Tianna Sicilia
APPLES FOR LOVE	57	Natalie J. Wilson
ROASTING HAZELNUTS	59	Tianna Sicilia
CRYSTAL GRID FOR SELF-LOVE	60	Michael Herkes
ROSE QUARTZ BATH	62	Kiki Dombrowski
VIOLETS FOR LOVE	63	Natalie J. Wilson
STIMULATE LUSTFUL ENERGY	64	Michael Herkes
WITCH HAZEL FOR LOVE	65	Natalie J. Wilson
EXERT SEXUAL PRIDE CRYSTAL GRID	66	Michael Herkes
PET LOVE	69	Rebecca Ferreira Troy
AMBER FOR ATTRACTION	70	Kiki Dombrowski

CONTENTS

COME AND SEE ME OIL 71 Kiki Dombrowski

STONE FOR VALENTINE'S DAY 73 Michael Herkes

PART III
DIVINATION

☽ 75 ☾

INTRODUCTION 76 Kiki Dombrowski

THREE LUGGIES 81 Kiki Dombrowski

CHOOSE BETWEEN LOVERS 82 Tonya A. Brown

FLOWER DIVINATION 84 Kiki Dombrowski

MOON MAGIC AND PSYCHIC DREAMS 87 Kiki Dombrowski

LOVE IN PALMISTRY 88 Kiki Dombrowski

THE PENDULUM 91 Daina Renton

FOLK DIVINATION WITH HERBS 92 Kiki Dombrowski

ST. LUKE'S VERSE 93 Kiki Dombrowski

LOVE DIVINATION WITH TAROT 94 Kiki Dombrowski

DIVINING FIRE 97 Kiki Dombrowski

APPLES AND SAMHAIN 98 Kiki Dombrowski

CONTENTS

CELEBRATE LOVE TAROT SPREAD	100	Kiki Dombrowski
OMENS OF WEATHER	101	Kiki Dombrowski
CANDY HEART DIVINATION	102	Michael Herkes
TWO LOVERS TRIANGLE SPREAD	105	Kiki Dombrowski
LOVE INSIGHT	106	Tonya A. Brown
MIRRORS	107	Rebecca Ferreira Troy
LOVE DIVINATION CRYSTAL KIT	108	Kiki Dombrowski
PULL THE STALK	111	Kiki Dombrowski

PART IV
KITCHEN WITCH SPELLS
☽ 113 ☾

INTRODUCTION	114	Kiki Dombrowski
ALLURE THROUGH TASTE	117	Michael Herkes
HOW TO CREATE A LOVING MEAL	118	Andrea Maldonado
PASSION CHARM	121	Em Miiller
DIY PASSION CANDLES	122	Tonya A. Brown
LOVE SPELL COOKIES	123	Tianna Sicilia

CONTENTS

LUSTCRAFT POTION	124	Michael Herkes
SIMPLE LOVE POTION	126	Natalie J. Wilson
BLUE MOON INCENSE	127	Kiki Dombrowski
PROTECT LOVE CHARM	128	Michelle Denison
FAIRY WINE	129	Tonya A. Brown
ROSY LOVE OIL FOR JUNE	131	Kiki Dombrowski
UNITING WITH WINE RITUAL	132	Mary Elisabeth Young
EROTIC ECLAIRS	134	Tonya A. Brown
LUXURIOUS BODY MOISTURIZERS	137	Emma Kathryn
THE LOVERS' ROSE SALVE	138	Effy Winter
ATTRACTION OIL	139	Kiki Dombrowski
STRAWBERRY AND CHOCOLATE FACE MASK	140	Emma Kathryn
LOVING HERBAL STICK	141	Kiki Dombrowski
FACIAL TONIC FOR ATTRACTION	143	Em Dobbins
HOT CHOCOLATE FOR A LOVING HOME	144	Tonya A. Brown
DRAW LOVE FLOOR WASH	146	Emma Kathryn

CONTENTS

MEAL TO MEND STRAINED RELATIONSHIPS 148 Tonya A. Brown

COOKING MAGIC FOR LOVE 150 Andrea Maldonado

PART V
DIETY WORK

☽ 153 ☾

INTRODUCTION 154 Amanda Wilson

HONOURING JUNO 159 Em Miiller

BEAUTY 160 Kiki Dombrowski

FERTILITY 161 Kiki Dombrowski

ATTRACTING ROMANCE 163 Kiki Dombrowski

LOVE ALTAR 165 Rebecca Ferreira Troy

CELEBRATE LOVE 167 Kiki Dombrowski

☽ ☉ ☾

CONCLUSION 168 Emma Kathryn

CONTRIBUTORS 170

FOREWORD

I remember from a young age that the idea of falling in love felt like the ultimate act of magic. The thought of love seemed to be absolute bliss and I could not wait for the chance to experience it myself. Maybe this came from being the product of fairytale culture. Growing up, I absolutely loved watching movies or hearing fairytales, so the ideas of true love and happily ever after were cemented in my mind from adolescence. But the interesting thing is that in most cases there was a witch at the center of the story being sought for their ability to bewitch, attract, and even end relationships. Perhaps that is one of the subconscious reasons I became a witch. I mean why find one to enchant your love life when you can become a witch yourself and transform your life with all acts of love and pleasure?

FOREWORD

The first spell I ever cast was a "Come to Me" love spell. I wrote all of the components I wanted to find in a partner on a piece of paper with a red pen, placed it under a pink candle and allowed the wax to melt down on it. I then placed the dried charm into my backpack in hopes of drawing a love to me. It did not happen right away, but several years down the line my true love came to me and it was as if I saw life in new color—everything was more vivid and I was in a complete state of euphoria. I felt as though I had moved from earth to cloud nine where I was constantly floating. Perhaps it was even more ecstatic because I experienced the sour pain of rejection many times before that of love. But it was from this experience that I also learned that like a rose, love builds up, blooms, endures, and eventually fades back from whence it came only to be reborn in another fashion. I can remember my first spell to heal a broken heart almost as vividly as the one that got me there.

Love is beautiful and love is dark. Love can heal, causing peace and compassion, but it is also a war that can cause much pain and anguish. It is neither black nor white—just like witchcraft. There is power in the duality of feelings that stem from love, yet I believe that the true magic of a witch is love—how to absorb, reflect, heal, and cast it out into the universe. A witch is more powerful when their heart is fully open, being of service to the community around them, and attracting all aspects of love.

This book is a compendium for love magic—not just finding it in someone else but also in yourself. Whether you use the spells and rituals here in their full context or as inspiration for your own magic, remember that all is full of love and you as a witch are a catalyst for it to grow and flow all around you. This book gives you the tools to color your life with all of the shades of love. May you find the love within and let it blossom into the world…attracting more and more love to you like a flower does the bee.

Blessed be!
–Michael Herkes, *The Glam Witch*

INTRODUCTION

Love spells are often the first thing newer witches reach for when stepping into the world of magic. I did too! No judgment. However, this is not a book that will teach you magic. Witchcraft, casting, and magic are a lifelong journey and there are many books out there that will give you a solid foundation on how to get started. This book is meant to be a reference guide for witches drawn to the sweeter spells in life. A collection of spells ranging from simple to complex from various witches around the world. Something to pluck from your bookshelf when you're feeling unsure, curious, saucy, or sexy. Though, what witchcraft book would this be if I didn't break down a little about how spells work?

PREFACE

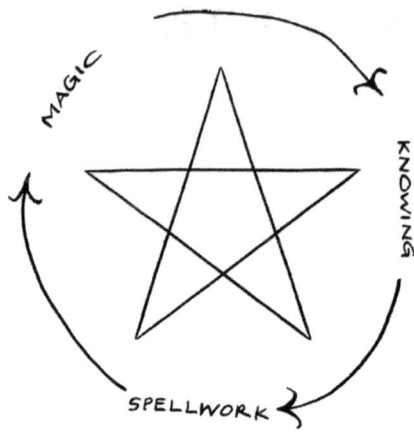

"The Cycle of Witchcraft" is something I coined in *The Door to Witchcraft*. This is the cycle in which an idea enters our mind, we decide that magic must be done, we cast, then the magic manifests.

Here is an excerpt from *The Door to Witchcraft*:

> *The Cycle is as follows: Knowing - Witchcraft - Magic*
>
> *Knowing: Having a clear and concise idea of what needs to change. The first part of creating magic is being aware of yourself, your space, and those around you. A witch may use a form of divination to determine what's going on if they don't already know. They may use cards, meditate for information, or ask spirit guides.*
>
> *Witchcraft: Taking action to create change. It is at this point that the witch needs to determine the best course of action. What you decide to do is based off your magical niche, your instinct about what is best, and what you know about the situation.*
>
> *Magic: Change created. Energy is shifted and begins to work. Magic typically works from the witch out, into the world.*

This book gives you a little bit of each stage of The Cycle of Witchcraft. To *know* you may choose to divine - our divination section will give you multiple ways that you can choose to gain more information. To *craft* is to do spell work, each section of this book will give you actionable ideas for spells, rituals, and other forms of witchcraft. Finally, *magic* - now magic is not just about a spell manifesting, but about creating a space around you where spells *can* manifest. The affirmation shared at the beginning of each section will give you tips for how to create a healthy and happy relationship with yourself and those around you. Essays before each section will give you a little food for thought and more information on love spells and the magic around them.

Now it's a cycle - so that means we may keep circling around. Once a spell is cast and the magic manifests it is up to the witch to determine if the results are what was wanted and expected. Knowing will give you the opportunity to tap into yourself to determine if what you truly want and need is what is occurring post spell work. If so, you can break the cycle, if not, it's time to gear up for another trip around the circle.

Witches, I hope you enjoy this little book of love magic and that you find it to be a guide to living deliciously.

–Tonya A. Brown, *Editor*

PART I
RITUAL SPELLS

PART I

INTRODUCTION
LOVE SPELLS & FREE WILL

When I hear the words "love spell" my hackles usually go up. This is my knee-jerk reaction to what, for me, brings up thoughts of controlling other people, something I am usually staunchly against. Recently, however, with some perspective and guidance, I am reassessing that reaction. It was a bit of a come to Lilith moment, if you know what I mean, when my friend and editor urged me to think beyond my own preconceptions. To think of love spells as solely having a romantic or sexual goal is frankly outdated (though I will address this later). Love magic is layered and can be quite subtle, like a good bottle of wine, or maybe your favorite perfume.

I'm partial to looking back into our history for answers. I find it helpful in all aspects of thought to know where we were in order to figure out where we are going. The topic of love spells is no different. One example might be found in some of the magics from Ancient Greece. Magic appears to have been rather widely practiced, across all classes. It seems that even men were known to cast spells of an amorous and sexual nature, attempting to gain the affections and attentions of those whom they desired; that magic is commonly known as "eros" magic, named for the Greek god of love himself, Eros. Housewives of the time, on the other hand, appear to have been fond of practicing philia magic. Philia is often interpreted as "brotherly love" or deep fondness; the aim was affection, not desire. In a time and society where women were considered inferior and found themselves at the complete mercy of their husbands, might it not be understandable to attempt to bring about an amicable relationship? I have read, however, that this form of magic was often looked down upon by men of the time, as they considered it a form of manipulation. I mean, how dare these women engage in acts to create a safe and loving space for themselves, right? I hope you see the deep irony here. As I understand it, the Greeks had four types of love magic, the other two being storge (a familial love) and agape (a selfless and unconditional love). While there are myriad traditions, practices, and viewpoints on magic (and thank goodness for that!), I quite like the simplicity of this four-part concept.

So let's think about this idea of philia. In this context, the word refers to fondness and friendliness. In modern times we often hear it as a suffix indicating a tendency toward things (the antonym of philia is phobia, coming from the Greek word phobos, meaning fear or horror). However, as I understand it, philia magic is intended to create an environment of support, respect, and admiration. I think this is something even non-magical people are striving for in their lives regularly. Think about buying your partner's favorite bottle of wine to share at dinner. Consider the simple act of pouring your intentions of love and partnership along with the wine as you fill their glass. Might this not be a love spell, perhaps even a potion? I would wager this act is one of generosity and hope, not one of manipulation.

This leads me to consider a recent moment in my kitchen. My child was unwell, laying on the couch and clutching his tummy in near agony. All

PART I

I wanted was to bring him comfort, to soothe his pain and bring him rest. As I worked, sprinkling herbs into a bowl to prepare a cup of tea to ease his discomfort, I chanted, "bring him ease and let him rest," over and over again as it steeped, as I added honey, as I stirred it for him. I watched him as he sipped, sending him all my loving intention. Soon, he drifted off to sleep and when he awoke, his tummy ache was a distant memory. This is a form of love magic. This is what might be classified under the Greek term storge, a familial love. Or might it be also be an example of agape, as any parent knows our love for our children comes from a deep and unconditional source within us. This certainly is not a love felt only by parents, though, as it is about family (those we create as well as those we are born into). Another wonderful example of agape magic that does not infringe upon anyone else's will would be anything having to do with healing our planet. I once knew a witch who made it her mission to work toward easing or dispersing the earthquakes in California. Her entire goal was just to keep her statewide community safe. This was a selfless, loving magic.

Leaving the Greeks and their ideas aside, I find my mind pondering the idea of self-love. I would be a liar if I claimed to be unfamiliar with the power and healing and magic of self-love, as well as self-care. I have, in fact, almost entirely based my own magical practice on it. I have taught classes on it for years and have witnessed the incredible effects it has to offer. In a world that regularly seeks to diminish our power by creating unrealistic beauty expectations, places value on us by our productivity and income, or even the number of "likes" we get on social media posts, it can often be difficult to live in self-love. Please let me tell you this one thing right now, and then we can get back to the love magic: you are spectacular. You are beautiful in your favorite hoodie and with your messy hair. All the things about you that you see as flaws are your glorious, unique, divine qualities. You only need to see that and own it. This is what self-love magic is all about.

Out of all forms of love spells and magic, the practice of self-love magic is, to me, the most powerful and the least intrusive. Every other form of love magic is aimed at others (even my tummy ache tea magic noted above with its healing intention). Self-love magic infringes in no way, shape, or form on another person, with the possible exception of you loving yourself and your divine power so much that you choose to excise people in your life who would bring you down or wish you ill. One of my favorite spells for self-love involves slathering myself head to toe with a sugar scrub imbued with love. While I do this, I consider what I love about myself. I remind myself that I am a glorious, divine creature, filled with magic. Additionally, considering the exfoliating action of the sugar as I circle it into my flesh, I release my self-doubt and judgment. I slough it away and let it swirl down the drain with my dead skin. In the end, I am renewed, glowing, and invigorated. This type of love magic can also be seen in works for healthy boundaries. It might look like generating a shield of protection around yourself, crafting a sachet or an amulet to carry with you for protection, or perhaps even a simple mantra you work in your head throughout a particularly challenging day. It is aimed at creating a safe and sacred space for and within yourself and is absolutely self-love magic.

As I am typing this, I find myself considering glamour magic. I think this might be one of the most commonly practiced acts of love magic out there; though I'd bet many people don't even realize that's what it is. It can be both an act of self-protection and one of self-worship. On one hand, how many times have I been experiencing a bad day filled with low self-esteem, poor body image, and general imposter syndrome only to decide to don my favorite shawl, anoint myself in oils, and slick a gleaming gloss across my lips in order to remind myself just who the hell I am? The answer—many, many times. I bet I am not alone in this practice. Anyone else in this club with me? It is why makeovers are so popular. It is a rebirth, a reimagining, or a reembracing of our glory! On the other hand, the act of self-worship through glamour magic . . . oh, that's my jam! Anyone who knows me could tell you that this is part of my regular practice. There is something divine, for me, in the purposeful practice of donning my favorite clothing and adornments, painting my face to suit whatever mood I am in, and dancing to a favorite song in front of a mirror (and quite possibly taking far too many photos of myself). To be fed power by my own reflection, in honor of the divine magic within me, is like charging up a battery. It fills me with a sizzling sensation of potential and power. Still, I would venture to say that glamour magic can be as simple as a spritz of your favorite perfume or as complex as ritual bathing and anointing your body beneath the moon. It is up to you what the act looks like, but the outcome is pretty much universally empowering.

I feel that I would be remiss, however, not to address another kind of love magic, one that I mentioned earlier that is aimed at capturing the "love" or infatuation of another person. Is it a time honored part of the practice of magic? Or a dangerous way to strip another person of their will? While these are answers we must all arrive at on our own, I have a pretty strong opinion on the matter. I am going to give you my opinion. Are you ready for it? Here goes. Love spells can be very dangerous, and I am not in favor of their practice in this regard, generally. I know, it can be an unpopular opinion. Let me explain. When I hear the words "love spell," what I often interpret them as is "I want to make this person love me, despite what they may or may not want." Now I ask you, does that sound like a good idea to you? We're talking about free will here, or rather the removal of it. I think we have all seen or read more than enough examples in fiction of love spells gone wrong and then resulting in single-minded obsession or worse. It may be fiction, but they are onto something, I'd say. Besides, you are worth so much more than the mindless rapture of an ensnared minion, don't you think?

All that being said, I am not without my own attempts. Full disclosure, the first spells I ever tried were love spells. I think that can be said for many of us. How many red or pink candles did I clumsily dress and burn in my teens? I lost count. In fact, I can clearly remember being 16 years old and sneaking out to a rose garden at midnight with the intention to cast a powerful love spell. There was a guy that I had the biggest crush on. He was a few years older than me, and while we were close friends, he had made it pretty clear that our relationship would go no further. Undeterred, I set my mind to making him mine. I had stolen a necklace from my mother to enchant. It had been a perfume-holding necklace from Avon that had dried out long ago, the perfect vessel. I walked through the garden, plucking one single petal from each rose that caught my eye. I would then mash the petals into the necklace, followed by one of my adolescent tears, repeatedly chanting "he will love me." I wore it around my neck the entire summer. Every time I saw him I would hold it, my eyes locked on him, wondering if this would be the moment my spell would come to life, waiting for him to look at me with eyes glazed with magical enchantment and desire. Of course, he never did. He soon left the orbit of my life, but I still have the necklace. Looking at it now, it is a sweet teenage memory, but what if it had worked? What if I had ensnared him despite him not actually having feelings for me? What might that have looked like? I am glad I did not have to find out.

This is the questionable aspect of love magic: impeding the free will of another individual. Is it even love if all parties involved are not there willingly? Records of love spells have been found dating back centuries. The oldest known love spells have been found in the ancient Near East, what we refer to as Mesopotamia (modern-day Iraq). These tablets are over 4,000 years old and are commonly referred to as cuneiform or curse tablets. They have been found to contain spells for a variety of love-related magics, some as simple as familial blessings and marital arrangements, and others pertaining to erotic objects and divorce instructions. I do not know enough about them to judge their full intent, but I find it fascinating that humans thought to cast for love all those centuries ago, and I can't help but wonder what came from those attempts. There are Egyptian love spells written on papyrus dating back to the third century, calling to "burn the heart" of a woman until the caster's love is returned (according to translator Franco Maltomini from the University of Udine in Italy). In most of these instances, we find that spells for love were aimed at capturing the heart or mind of someone who might otherwise be unwilling. There are, however, exceptions to this in other instances. The line can seem a bit blurry, no? As with much magic, there is rarely a clear-cut black-and-white answer.

If you find yourself looking for love in your life, perhaps consider working some of the aforementioned self-love magic. I am partial to bathing away self-doubt, moisturizing with love-infused oils, and solo sex magic aimed at creating an aura of desire around myself. These are for me and by me, but they certainly can achieve the desired effect of attraction, all without attempting to infringe upon the will of another. I wish you so much abundance and fortune as you explore these ideas and work toward love.

–Michelle Guerrero Denison, *Writer*

Enjoy All Kinds of Love

Love isn't just a romantic comedy. Love comes in all forms. You love your family, your pet, your friends, your coven, and yourself. Whether you are in a relationship or not, recognize that loving relationships are not just limited to the romantic kind.

— Kiki Dombrowski

RITUAL SPELLS

ATTRACT COMMITMENT

If you have an abundant outlook, your heart is open, and you are a vessel for self-love, a person worthy of committing to you will come into your space. Alternatively, your current partner will be encouraged to raise their energy frequency. Think "beauty" in everything you do. Set the intention for a mature, committed love to enter your life. Make everything a conduit for loving energy.

Remember, as you begin to stand strong in your energy the universe might grant your wish for a monogamous relationship in ways you didn't expect, so be open, have fun, and most of all, believe you are worthy, and the universe will respond!

CANDLE SPELL

✦

Adorn a pink candle with rose or patchouli essence.

☾

Burn slowly every evening until the moon is full.

✸

You can build an altar for yourself with items that remind you that you are worthy of what you are seeking; a charged lapis lazuli gem, for instance, is a gem known for love, abundance, and fidelity.

PART I

GLAMOUR WITH SIGHT

It goes without saying that glamour magic has a lot to do with appearance. While this is partially true, outer appearance works in tandem with your inner confidence in glamour magic. For this sense, you will use your bewitchment to project your seduction goals! To do this, you have to first worship yourself.

✦

Start by lighting some red candles in your bathroom. Take a sexy bath with your favorite bath bomb or body scrub (if you aren't a bath kind of gal/guy, a shower is fine) and really indulge yourself. Light some incense, add some rose petals and damiana (both powerful herbs of attraction and love/lust), and a few tumbled carnelian (sexuality and vitality) and garnet (sensuality and confidence) crystals into the water. Hear the soft sexy beats from your mix in the background. Seduce yourself. It all starts within you.

☾

Once your bath is finished, dry off and start getting ready. Don't rush through this part. Take your time. Select one of your favorite outfits. Something that really makes you feel confident in yourself. Use color magic when selecting your outfit. Dress yourself in rich reds or hot pinks. Something that really is electrifying, that drips with sexiness. As an added kick, you can use crystal magic through jewelry to help amplify results. Your best bet would be to use red, pink, or orange colored crystals that exude sensuality and confidence like carnelian, garnet, red tiger's eye, ruby, bloodstone, rhodonite, rhodochrosite, or rose quartz.

✺

When it comes to sight, also remember that "eyes are the windows to the soul." Make sure you have proper eye contact with your partner throughout the night. Eye contact is an important form of communication highlighting confidence and affirming attention.

RITUAL SPELLS

CONJURE LOVE

Hold the intention of supreme love coming into your life. Never be afraid to be specific. It is your future love, so be sure of exactly what you want.

CANDLE SPELL

List the type of love you want on a piece of paper. Place the paper under your pillow on the new moon. Remove the paper on the full moon and burn it, returning your wants to the universe. Watch them manifest.

☾

Choose a red or pink candle (passion/self-love), or use both candles. After all, true love is attracted to self-love. Friday is an excellent day to perform love magic.

✴

You can utilize oils, I love orange oil (for joy as well as love), ylang-ylang or geranium are excellent too.

☽

Call in the elements as you open your circle, and make sure to articulate the specifics of what you desire when you work within your spell. Don't forget to close your circle, and thank the elements for aiding you in your quest for love.

REBECCA FERREIRA TROY — OCTOBER 2017

PART I
❖HOW TO BOND WITH A SPIRIT LOVER AND FAMILIAR❖

STEP 1
After crafting a flying ointment for sensual hedgecrossing and allowing it to age in your cupboard, coat your body in the salve from head to toe, careful not to cover parts of your body that may be irritated by the ointment.

STEP 2
Find a place to relax and meditate—this can be in a dark bedroom or out in nature in the middle of the night (which I find works best). Close your eyes and concentrate on connecting your energy to the spirit you are wanting to bond with. During this time, the flying ointment will aid you in slipping into a trance-like state—you may begin lucid dreaming. Witches' flight can be achieved naturally but might require practice for some. Be patient with yourself. It is important to remember that you must let yourself go. Let your body dissolve around you and do not overthink this practice. Embrace the blackness that you see and feel your spirit fall away into another world.

STEP 3
When your spirit begins to leave your body, you will feel as if you are floating and all of your senses may be heightened. Oftentimes, the witch will see their physical body below them as they separate from it.

STEP 4
As you make your way through the veil to the Otherworld, take care not to follow clouded areas that feel unsafe. Understand that there are risks that come with spirit flight— many things exist in this realm. Always protect yourself and call upon your guides if you need them.

STEP 5
After bonding with your spirit lover in the Otherworld, begin returning to the physical plane. Ease back into your body. Allow yourself to gently return to the world of the living and expect that you may feel light-headed from crossing between the veil. Make sure to wash off the flying ointment after spirit flight.

RITUAL SPELLS

NEW RELATIONSHIP COMMUNICATION

If the person you are seeing is invested in a future with you they will listen to you with an open heart. Ask open-ended questions; "How do you feel about being together exclusively?" or "What can we do to take this relationship to the next step?"

CANDLE SPELL

Light a yellow candle and anoint it
with almond oil or rosemary oil.

Say the following three times:

I am vulnerable, I am authentic.

I speak from my heart, I speak the truth.

I listen to understand, I respond to support.

Take the leap and speak to him or her
about what you want in the relationship before you try a magical remedy.

If he or she isn't responding with enthusiasm,
then it is time for you to reconsider whether he
or she is looking for the same thing romantically.

TIP

When looking for love of any kind, the best way to cast a spell without attempting to change the will of others is to not have a specific person in mind whose love you desire. Instead, cast a spell that will attract a person with the qualities you desire. As long as you are not attempting to put a spell on a person, you don't typically have to worry about affecting the will of another.

–Jessica Ripley

TRUE LOVE SPELL

SIMPLE SPELL

✦

Write a list by hand (do not type it) of all the attributes you're looking for in a lover, with an emphasis on character. How do you want to feel when you are with them? How do you want to be treated? What are the virtues you look for in a companion? Get specific.

☾

Then, seal your intention of attracting this person by saying:

As I will, so it is done.

The next part is hard—waiting.

✶

Be open, and allow this person to come to you. In the meantime, do not settle for suitors who don't fit your list of requirements. This will ensure that you receive what you've asked for.

JESSICA RIPLEY FEBRUARY 2018

PART I

✧ ENHANCE YOUR GLAM

YOU WILL NEED

- 3 black candles—remove negativity and unwanted habits
- 3 red tiger's eye crystals—for sensuality and courage
- 3 moonstone crystals—strengthen your inner light
- Compact mirror, preferably one that magnifies
- 3 pink candles—for inner peace and love
- 3 gold candles—for attraction and glow
- A pink figure candle—to represent you
- 3 rose quartz crystals—for self-love
- Rose oil—for beauty and grace
- Ginger oil—for confidence
- Piece of paper and a pen
- Multicolor glitter
- A fireproof dish

> Before getting started in the circle take time to make yourself feel luxurious and glamorous. A face mask, a bath, candles, champagne? Whatever it takes to raise your confidence.

STEP 1

Once ready, create a large circle with the first six items listed above. Light your candles and step inside the circle. Create your sacred space in whatever way you prefer. Write out the qualities you like most about yourself on the paper.

STEP 2

Carve your name into the figurine candle and seal it by either pricking or licking your finger and wiping it over the carving. Anoint the candle with three drops of each oil and dowse it with the glitter to intensify the glamour. Channel your energies into the candle. Become one with it. Light your figurine candle and say:

Sacred flame, burning bright, set my soul ablaze and let my glamour ignite.

MICHAEL HERKES   JANUARY 2018

STEP 3

Set your list on fire from the flame of the candle and say,

> *May these traits*
> *within me*
> *radiate stronger*
> *and be set free.*

Place the burning paper into the dish to turn into ash.

STEP 4

Next, open the compact and say the following:

> *Tiny mirror of mine,*
> *let my confidence and*
> *glamour shine. Reflect the*
> *best qualities in me, and*
> *magnify them for all to see.*
> *For the good of all,*
> *but most for me,*
> *As I will it,*
> *so shall it be.*

Leaving the compact open, turn it upside down and place on the plate. Sprinkle the ashes of your list onto the back of the compact, then pour the wax from your figurine candle on top of it as well. You do not need to burn out the entire candle. Pour just enough wax to cover the ash and seal it to the back of the compact, charging the mirror inside with your glamorous intent.

STEP 5

Once the wax has cooled, look into the compact and see yourself as you want to be seen. Take a mental snapshot of yourself now, in this state, and concentrate that into the mirror to look back on.

STEP 6

When you feel you are ready, you can end the ritual and go right to bed. Close the mirror and sleep with it under your pillow to charge and align with you while you sleep. Look back on it as often as needed whenever in doubt or when you need a bit of a glam boost. Save your candle for repeated use, for the next time you need to recharge! Now be sexy, hexy, and unleash your inner glam witch on the world!

PART I

TIP

You can tailor any spell to be less specific. "Come to Me" spells are great alternatives because they allow the universe to help encourage what is meant to harmoniously appear in your life. As for glamours, they are really about using yourself as a charm. They are not really designed to change someone else's will but more your own mindset in cultivating confidence and sexiness.

Attraction spells are good for bringing in love of any kind. Sometimes these are confused with glamours. Despite the name, the type of attraction spells I am talking about are not necessarily for superficial attraction or beauty. Instead, they help you to attract, or rather magnetize, whatever you desire, be it love, friendship, money, protection, etc.

–Michael Herkes

RITUAL SPELLS

COME TO ME

YOU WILL NEED
- Lavender
- 1 pink rose
- Elderflowers
- A piece of paper
- A red or pink pen
- 1 rose quartz crystal
- A pink drawstring bag
- 1 cauldron / fireproof dish
- 1 pink figure candle in the gender you desire

STEP 1
Perform this between the first quarter waxing and full moon as this is a potent time for new beginnings. Create a sacred space and prepare to begin. Hold your rose quartz crystal in your hand while you write down the qualities of a mate that you desire. A good mix would be physical and emotional characteristics, zodiac signs, ambitions, lines of work, etc. while remaining as general as possible.

STEP 2
Once your list is complete, place the rose quartz in front of the figure candle. Light it and say, *"Energies of the universe, hear me. I call for a love, a life partner they will be. Send to me my perfect mate. May I meet them and have our first date, Fall in love, and within time, He/She will become forever mine!"*

STEP 3
Set the paper on fire and place it in the dish to burn into ash. Sprinkle the ash onto the burning candle and visualize the qualities being absorbed into the candle. Envision the candle becoming the person that will be your true mate. Take your rose and pull the petals off one by one while chanting, *"come to me, come to me, come to me,"* over and over to raise the power.

STEP 4
Place them into your pink bag with the other herbs. Elderflowers are great for drawing love, and lavender is great for luck. Set the bag aside. The candle will need to burn for a few hours until it is burnt completely out. Make sure that this is done safely.

STEP 5
Once the candle is out, wax should have formed on the plate around the crystal. Gather the wax drippings and crystal and place it in the pouch you created. Carry the bag with you until the love you asked for comes to you.

MICHAEL HERKES   OCTOBER 2017

PART I

EXPLORE LOVE INCANTATIONS

TO EXPLORE WHAT THE MEANING OF LOVE IS IN YOUR LIFE REPEAT THE FOLLOWING INCANTATION:

To understand true love
I explore thee,
I explore thee,
I am open to authentic love,
as I desire, so mote it be.

TO WELCOME IN PLATONIC LOVE AND FRIENDSHIP REPEAT THE FOLLOWING INCANTATION:

To enjoy platonic love
I celebrate thee,
I celebrate thee,
I make friends easily,
as I desire, so mote it be.

KIKI DOMBROWSKI   MARCH 2019

RITUAL SPELLS

STRENGTHEN NON-ROMANTIC LOVE

YOU WILL NEED
- Lavender—love and protection
- Sage or palo santo—cleansing
- A vessel to burn loose incense in
- Clear quartz—to raise vibrations
- 2 pink candles—1 for you and 1 for the person you wish to bond with (pink = friendship)
- The person you wish to strengthen your bond with, in person if possible, or a picture of that person
- Passion flower—attract friendship
- Amethyst—to provide help in strengthening your bond
- Rose petals—for close and lasting relationships
- Lime rind or essential oil—to strengthen love
- Matches or a lighter
- Any other items you regularly use with spellwork
- ☾ Feel free to substitute ingredients

STEP 1
We will start by gathering all of your items and setting up your workspace. You will need the person you are wishing to strengthen your bond with, either in person or in a picture. You will need two pink candles as close to each other as possible. Place your vessel for the incense as well. This is where you will place your rose petals, passion flower, and lime. You can place the amethyst and quartz wherever you feel is necessary. You may also place any other items that you feel you need or want for the spell.

STEP 2
When you are finished setting up, cleanse the workspace. After this, you will light the candles and incense, then begin.

STEP 3
You can either silently repeat your intention or say it aloud. If you need guidance, consider saying something like:

We ask to strengthen our bond of love and friendship.

Just concentrate on your intention of the spell. If you would like to call upon a god or goddess, you can ask for their help in this request as well. You may continue until the candles burn out, or you can work a little each day, whichever you feel most comfortable with.

NESSA SKINNER — FEBRUARY 2018

TIP

I love a good bath! Bath Bouquets are the perfect tool for relaxation and self-care. In this modern world, most people shower because bathing is seen as a luxury we just don't have time for anymore. Well, I say bring back the bath! Yes, they might use a lot of water, but you won't be doing this daily, only every once in a while, so take the time to indulge. Use herbs and flowers for whatever you need. Chamomile, rose petals, lavender, thyme, rosemary... the choices are endless. All of these ingredients will promote feelings of relaxation and happiness. Tie them up in a muslin cloth and add to your running water.

–Emma Kathryn

RITUAL SPELLS

 ROSE RITUAL

Humans desire to hold on to our beauty. We grasp at it, reluctant to give up its power. As such it's only natural that we have a long history of preserving rose petals and incorporating them in our lives. These delicate, yet beautiful dried rose petals permeate our homes, championing our control over decay.

The rose, such exquisite beauty is made even more profound due to its impermanence. A few days of heightened refinement surround your space when the flower is at its peak. Such delicate beauty is temporary.

YOU WILL NEED
+ ½ cup dried rose petals
+ 1-1½ cups epsom salts
+ ¼ cup baking soda
+ ½ cup sea salt

STEP 1
Place a cupful of this mixture in your bath water and reserve the rest for future use.

STEP 2
While bathing, visualize the essence of beauty seeping from the rose petals and swirling atop the water. Focus on your skin soaking in this essence and feel the light radiating through your body.

STEP 3
At the end of your bath, you will feel confident in your beauty and grace and ready to take on the world.

SCARLET RAVENSWOOD — JULY 2017

PART I

AMAS VERITAS

INSPIRED BY PRACTICAL MAGIC

The main spell of the movie is cast by a young girl named Sally while picking white rose petals in her family's greenhouse. She creates this spell for the "perfect" man because she knows that he will never exist.

She tells her younger sister, Gillian, "If he doesn't exist, then I'll never die of a broken heart" and she casts this spell, which she has written in her journal:

Summoning up a True-Love Spell: Amas Veritas

> He will hear my call from a mile away
> He will whistle my favorite song
> He can ride a pony backwards
> He can flip pancakes in the air
> He'll be marvelously kind
> And his favorite shape
> Will be a star
> And he'll have one green eye
> And one blue

Sally places the rose petals amongst small white flowers in a large wooden bowl as she recites the spell, and it is cast.

RITUAL SPELLS

> As an herbal ingredient, rose petals can be used to calm and soothe the mind and body, as well as strengthen the immune system and heal wounds. Ailments that can be amplified with stressful emotions are good candidates to be treated with rose petals.

You can do this spell too! Simple spells can often be the best spells, provided that our intentions are pure and true and that we are willing to be patient. Sally's true-love spell ingredients are only white rose petals and a few smaller white flowers, both of which are powerful additions to a spell.

The white rose representing innocence and purity used in this spell is countered later in the film, as we see an evil entity who creates a growth of dark red roses. White roses are said to take on the color and power of the emotion evoked in a spell. Their power to change with emotions also allows them to alter those emotions when paired with honest intention, making them one of the most effective ingredients that we can use in a spell of emotion.

YOU WILL NEED
+ A large wooden bowl
+ Small white flowers
+ White rose petals
+ Pen and paper

> White roses have not only medicinal properties as an herb but magical properties that have been documented over thousands of years. A typical wild rose has five main petals and five sepals, each representing a point on the pentagram: earth, air, water, fire, and spirit.

STEP 1
To create this spell on your own, rewrite the qualities of the person you are evoking so they cater to your own desires.

STEP 2
Add white rose petals to a large wooden bowl while reciting the spell. Add small white flowers of your choice to further employ the magic of purity to your spell.

STEP 3
Patience is essential, as is our continuous positive energy toward the spell. Everything comes to those who wait.

PART I

RELATIONSHIP STRENGTH

YOU WILL NEED
- A knife
- A ziplock bag
- A fireproof dish
- Clear packing tape
- A single photo of you
- A single photo of them
- 1 black candle between 5-7"
- 2 pink figure candles to represent each of you

> Love spells that are tied directly to someone can backfire—the person may become overly needy, destructive, or you might find that you just aren't into them!

STEP 1
Begin by creating your sacred space. Take the knife and carve your name (or initials) into the candle that represents you. Prick or lick your finger and drag it over the carving to seal it with your energies. Carve your lover's name into the candle that represents them.

STEP 2
Take your knife and chip away at the bottom of the black candle until the wick is exposed. You will be lighting the candle upside down to reverse the negative energies that stand between the two of you. In the fireproof dish, place the two photos next to each other. Place your candle on your photo and their candle on theirs. Between the figure candles place the black candle.

STEP 3
Light the figure candles. Focusing on the connection between the two of you, say *"May our lives combine and grow, as this candle burns and wax begins to flow. It will join us together now with infinite tomorrows!"* Next light the black candle and say *"Blackest candle, ignite and cast away. All negativity so that you will only see me. And likewise, may my eyes not wander, And our love will grow significantly fonder!"*

STEP 4
Let the candles burn and form together. Once they have burned out, take the wax and wrap it with the tape. While wrapping say *"With intentions pure and true, may you only love me and I you, together we are now combined, committed to each other for this lifetime."* Place your creation into a Ziplock bag and fill it halfway with water. Lock the bag and place it deep in the freezer for no one to ever find.

MICHAEL HERKES   OCTOBER 2017

SELF-CARE RITUAL

This is a great way to spend some much needed time for yourself. It is helpful in clearing/balancing our energy and allows us to release things that are no longer serving us.

STEP 1
First, lay down and put your right hand on top of your head at your crown chakra (it will stay here for the remainder of the ritual.) Take a moment to connect your vibration and relax into your body. Take notice of your rhythmic breathing.

STEP 2
Once you feel open and ready to continue, place your left hand over your third eye. Try to feel the humming of the energy that courses between your two hands. Picture violet waves of energy that flow back and forth cleansing your energetic field as it passes through.

STEP 3
Continue moving your left hand down the body to your throat chakra, picturing indigo waves of energy. (If you feel that you need to spend more time in any particular place, honor yourself by doing so.)

STEP 4
Next, place your left hand at your heart chakra picturing green energies flowing from back and forth. Then the solar plexus with yellow energies, Sacral with orange energies and the root with red.

STEP 5
Once you feel that all of these energies are balanced, picture a coiled snake at the base of your spine. See him slowly unwind himself and begin to travel up your spine. Wrapping himself around it, as he goes. Once he is fully extended, the ritual is complete.

PART I

SACRIFICE YOUR BROKEN HEART

YOU WILL NEED
+ Red pouch
+ Large plate
+ Kitchen twine
+ A black candle
+ Chocolate heart
+ Long stem rose with thorns
+ Blend of equal parts pink rose buds, elderberries/flowers, white sage, pine, cayenne, cinnamon, hibiscus, lavender
+ Charcoal disc in fireproof dish with sand
+ A pink candle for joy and happiness or red for romantic love, lust, desire

STEP 1
Cast circle or prepare for the spell in whatever manner you prefer. Once you are settled and grounded, take your chocolate heart and slice it down the center on your large plate. Ground yourself. Say:

I call upon (Dark Goddess of your choice),
I sacrifice my heart to you upon this night!
This carnal flesh and fragrant blooms,
Offerings to you on this dark moon,
So that the wound inside my chest
May finally be put to rest
And transformed into a gate
In which I will finally
Meet my fate.

STEP 2
Sprinkle some of the herbal blend onto a lit charcoal disc and scatter the rest into the pocket you have carved in the heart and recite these words:

Herbs of release and,
Herbs of banishment,
Herbs of love and luck,
Remove the pain that I harbor
So that I no longer give a fuck!

STEP 3

Remove the petals from the rose. Push the thorns from the stem into the mojo bag, scattering the petals over it saying:

Painful thorns, feel my anger and scorn.

Lush petals, heal my pain and forlorn.

The time has come to end my mourn.

May my heart be reborn!

STEP 4

Take the black candle and carve what you are releasing (pain, sadness, unrealistic expectations, prudence, inhibitions, etc.). Also, chip away at the bottom of the candle until the wick is exposed. You will be lighting it on this end so that it burns backwards for release. On the pink candle carve your name.

> These two candles are to act as a yin and yang. If you are releasing pain (black candle), then you will naturally be welcoming happiness (pink candle).

STEP 5

Cut two small grooves into the bag so that the small candle can rest in them. Say:

Sacred flames, on this night,

Heal my heart with all your might

The place inside where shadows dwell

Shall once again beam and swell

With the light that is so bright

And the chains that hold me back, strong and tight,

Shall finally be released

And my self-love will be increased.

STEP 6

Gaze into the flames and watch the
wax drip into the wounded heart. Say:

On this night I sacrifice my broken heart

And with it welcome a new start.

A chance to finally heal and grow

To ground and center, release and let go!

STEP 7

At this point you can continue to gaze into your fleshy poppet, meditate, cry, scream, let it all out! Do whatever you need to do to really feel the release. Open up and tell the dark goddess what it is that you need to release and why. But most importantly, let her know what you are going to do.

STEP 8

Once the candles have burned down, place
the chocolate heart in your poppet and say:

I purge myself of that which no longer

Serves and bless my heart with sweetness.

May my heart now be open and unbroken!

Take your twine and wrap it around your bag, sealing
it shut with all of the ingredients you have added to it.

STEP 9

If possible, leave your poppet out on your windowsill overnight so that it is charged by the dark moon. Upon waking the next morning discard it in one of two ways: 1) by tossing it into an open fire or more practically 2) burying it in the earth. Either way is a symbolic representation of letting go and releases the spell into the universe.

RITUAL SPELLS

FULL MOON SOULMATE RITUAL

YOU WILL NEED
+ Rose petals / rose essential oil
+ Cloves, rose, juniper, violet, and sandalwood herbs
+ Cauldron/incense burner
+ An object you think your soulmate would own
+ Your favourite perfume

It is best to do this on a full moon. It can be performed anytime, but this was effective on the day it was done, so we suggest the full moon. To prepare yourself and get into the frame of mind of the ritual you're about to perform, run yourself a bath and put in a few drops of rose essential oil (less is more) or just bathe in the rose petals themselves. If you can't have a bath, then washing your hands in rose water is a fine alternative.

STEP 1
Next, prepare your space and cast your circle as you always would. Sit in the centre of the circle and prepare your incense of cloves, rose, juniper, violet and sandalwood. These herbs are associated with love and enhance the spell. As the incense burns, pass the object through the smoke and imagine your soulmate coming into your life. When picking an object, simply think of what type of person your soulmate might be. If they're an artist for example, pass a paintbrush through the smoke. You'll know the right object for you.

STEP 2
As the incense burns further focus on the idea of your soulmate, what attributes you want in them, how they look, etc. Really think about it. You have to really want to meet them, so think about how much better your life will become once you meet. After 10 minutes or so of this, spray your favourite perfume on the object. People are attracted to smells, and this is a symbolic way of attracting that person to your smell.

STEP 3
Close your circle, and once done keep the ashes from the incense and place them in a bottle or sachet. A bonus addition to this ritual is if you ever meet that person who you believe could be them, give them the bottle to keep to solidify your bond and keep the love lasting. If you don't think you'd be able to give it to them, then keep it yourself.

DAINA RENTON

PART I

TURN FEAR INTO LOVE

STEP 1

Sit in front of two white candles, one to your left and one to your right, forming a triangle. If available to you, place a piece of obsidian nearby as well. As you light the first candle, think of yourself and your role in this ever-changing world we are all a part of. Remind yourself that you are powerful, courageous, and in charge of your life experience. Every choice that you make is an expression of this power. You are a goddess in your own right.

STEP 2

As you light the second candle, turn your attention to the world at large. Each of us is responsible for the role that we play. Your contribution is one drop in the vast sea of energy that binds us all together, whether we realize this bond or not. Think of the people that you call your allies. Think of the people that you want to show compassion toward and educate. How is your energy, their energies, and our collective energy changing?

STEP 3

Close your eyes, let your neck relax as your head bows, and simply feel the energetic ecosystem around you. We all have fears. We all want love. We want understanding, peace, and to feel safe. Love is all that truly exists between us.

STEP 4

Next, place your palms together in front of your abdomen, wherever they feel comfortable. Cross your thumbs and pull your palms apart to make a small triangle. Think of your linked hands as a steeple, a channel for your energy to flow through. When here, slowly open your eyes and gaze between the two candles, acknowledging the presence of both, at first as two pieces of a whole, then as two separate flames, then again as two pieces of a whole.

STEP 5

You are the good in the world. Channel love, as well as the empowerment it brings with it, through your steepled hands, into your belly. Picture it as a glowing yellow mist, surrounding you and protecting you. Remember, though, that you've created this. In turn, release any negativity that you may have been storing up. That anger, frustration, anxiety, and angst. Ask yourself where all of it came from. Is it fear? Is it a fear of a lack of love? Ask the universe to accept your negative thoughts and feelings, to take that potential energy and transform it, then release it.

EMME DICE　　　　　　　　　　　　　　　　　SEPTEMBER 2017

RITUAL SPELLS

HOODOO CANDLE MAGIC FOR ATTRACTING A LOVER

YOU WILL NEED
+ 1 pink lovers candle: male, couple, or ritual
+ 9 tablespoons sugar or 9 sugar cubes
+ 9½ teaspoons orange flower water
+ Dragon's blood or pink pen
+ 9 ½ teaspoons rose water
+ Mixing bowl & spoon
+ 9 teaspoons honey
+ Bowl for candle
+ Petition paper

STEP 1
Write your petition with your lover's name, or write "new love" and your name. Place on or under your bowl.

STEP 2
Mix your orange flower water, rose water, and honey together in a mixing bowl. Add the mix to your candle bowl. Next add the sugar to the mix. If you are using nine cubes, write your name and your lover's name on each cube.

STEP 3
Write your name and your lover's name on the pink candle. Write your command on the candle. Measure nine equal parts on the candle. Place in the center of the bowl.

> When you plan to do this spell, you may need to consider the moon phase and / or burn during the Venus hours. Start on a Sunday between 2 a.m. and 9 a.m. or 4 p.m. and 11 p.m. I prefer to do love spells during the times when people are typically sleeping.

STEP 4
Burn the candle during the Venus hours every day for nine consecutive days. Repeat candle magic spell for three weeks or when you feel called to perform this ritual. Dispose of your candle remains mindfully or bury in your front yard in a pink cloth.

HOODOO GODDESS — DECEMBER 2017

PART I

GET NOTICED

Sunstone can be utilized for love and glamour magic as well. The energetic heat from the stone can help purge negativity that has built up between partners or even rekindle the spark! As a fire stone, it can escalate passion in relationships, increasing sexual energy and stamina. Sunstone's warm, glowing nature also aligns with attraction. Wearing sunstone jewelry or carrying it in its tumbled form will increase your ability to get noticed, stand out from the crowd, entice potential mates, and even attract fame and fortune.

RITUAL SPELLS

BRING LOVE TALISMAN

VESSEL

Talismans are a really creative way to bring some magic into your life. As we are working with the intention of bringing love into the heart of the talisman wearer you might begin with two small pieces of red linen sewn together to make a pocket of sorts. You could also make or buy a small drawstring bag, that would work just as well. Red is the color of passion, and a romance fused with passion is ideal to me, but, if that doesn't suit you, the color pink would be an ideal choice.

HERBS

Next, I would add herbs traditionally associated with love: basil for joy (and money, success), thyme for affection, lavender for devotion, oregano for happiness and fennel for flattery. You don't need to use all of these herbs, but I included this list because for most of you kitchen witches out there they are herbs that are already lying around in your kitchen waiting to be utilized. If you don't have some of the herbs on hand a drop of aromatherapy oil would do the trick.

ADDITIONS

You could include a little heart, a pearl (associated with love), rose petals, or rose quartz; a gemstone that is associated with romantic love, self-love, and friendship. After all, you must love yourself first before you can truly love another.

SEAL

When you are finished adding what you desire to the talisman, seal it. I like to sew because I feel the energy tangibly fuses when I create the stitches. Do whatever feels right for you.

CHARGE

You can charge your Talisman in the same manner as you would your amulet or infuse a little candle magic into your desire to find love. You could use a pink candle on the corresponding day for love magic (Friday), with sandalwood, rose, or vanilla incense for added energy. Visualize the love you want to manifest and charge your talisman with that intention. The talisman can be kept on your person or under your pillow to influence your subconscious, freeing you from whatever energy could be holding you back from the love you desire and deserve.

REBECCA FERREIRA TROY · NOVEMBER 2016

PART I

MAGIC THROUGH TOUCH

While touch may seem like a really easy sense to work with when it comes to lustful endeavors there is a lot more to it than meets the eyes, or rather skin in this instance! This is the sense that allows you to really weave your magic and cast your spell. Sensual touch initiates a slew of sexual responses in our brains, and is a very effective communication tool.

✦

Touch is a sense that you should use all through the evening. Make an effort to flirtatiously touch your partner throughout the night. Don't just go straight for the cookie jar either! Leave a lingering touch that has your partner craving more. This could be as simple as a soft kiss where your lips barely meet. Softly caress the arm, barely touching, which will command the hairs on the back of the neck to jump up with excitement. Self-touch is an important element of this sense too. Use the art of body language to invite your partner and seduce them.

✷

Another element of touch to use is breath. Breath is a vital source of life. You can touch someone indirectly through the use of your breath. This is a fun and effective way to use lustcraft with touch. Breathing and blowing on your partner's fleshy erogenous zones are a surefire way to ignite passion between you!

RITUAL SPELLS

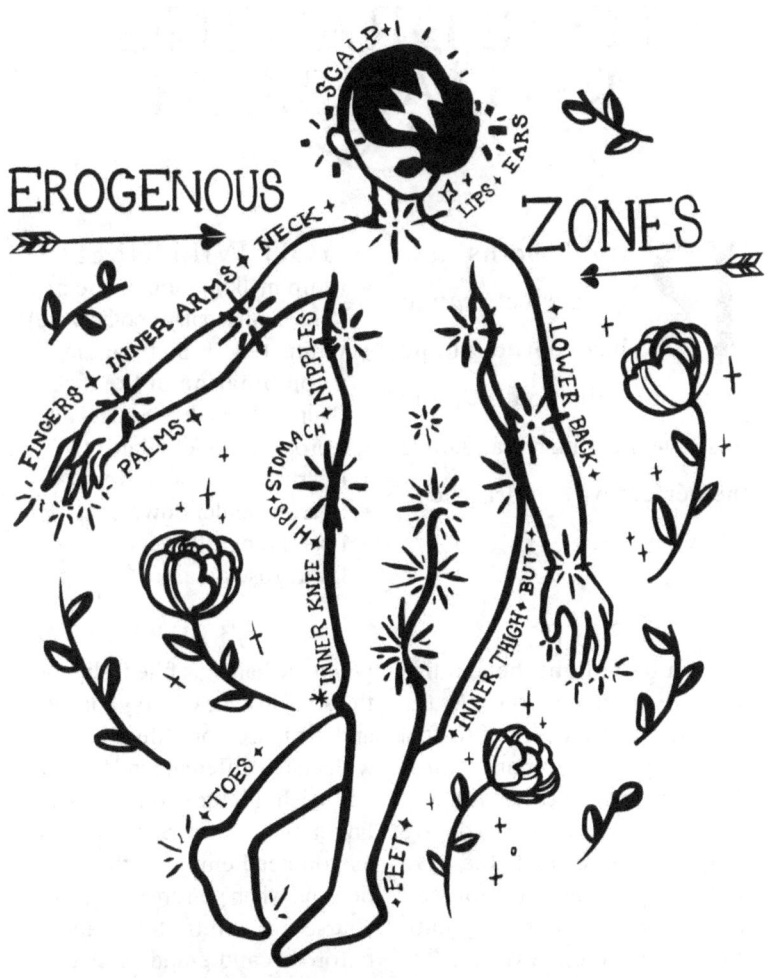

Erogenous zones are the areas on the body that have increased sensitivity. While the most known areas are the genitals, there are several others which can be seen above. Study the diagram to learn where you can touch your partner, and where you can tell them to touch you as well.

PART I

LOVE DRAWING RITUAL BATH

Ritual baths are the perfect way to incorporate magic into your daily routines and this love drawing ritual bath is the perfect way to draw love into your life.

YOU WILL NEED
+ 1 cup milk (you can use any kind of milk, dairy or otherwise)
+ White, red, or pink candles or a combination of the three
+ 10 drops lavender essential oil
+ 5 drops jasmine (dilute oil)
+ 1 part chamomile flowers
+ 1 part lavender flowers
+ 1 part jasmine flowers
+ 1 part rose petals

STEP 1
Draw a bath, light the candles and take off your clothes. As the bath fills allow yourself to feel love for you as you are. Know that you are perfect just the way you are. Acknowledge you are worthy of love. Feel the love and care you have for yourself spread through your body until it fills you completely.

STEP 2
Add the petals, milk and the oil to the water saying:

Love I want, I draw to me
As I will it so it shall be!

STEP 3
When the bath has filled, slip into the silky water. Close your eyes and visualise your life brimming with all the different kinds of love you wish. Picture yourself revelling in the feeling. Spend as long as you need enjoying the sensation and when you are ready, wrap yourself in a fluffy towel and sit before a candle and repeat the mantra. Take time enjoying the routine of taking care of yourself. Rub luxurious creams or oils into your skin and slip into your favourite nightwear, all the time knowing you are worthy of love and you will achieve all you desire.

EMMA KATHRYN

RITUAL SPELLS

MAGIC MIRROR LOVE SPELL

YOU WILL NEED
+ Mirror
+ Pink candle
+ Your favorite love oil or musk oil
+ Lipstick or marker for writing on the mirror

STEP 1
This spell is meant to help you see where love is in your life more clearly. Think about what love means to you, and write those descriptions about what love is on the mirror - you can write as many as you can fit or a few very valuable ones.

STEP 2
Anoint the candle with the oil and light it in front of the mirror.

STEP 3
Look into the mirror and say the following incantation:

Love is present,
Love is clear.
I see love and
I acknowledge it here.
May this mirror help me see
Where there is love in my life,
So mote it be.

Don't fret if you haven't found that right romantic partner or lusty situation that you are craving for the moment. A little patience may allow you to encounter the right situation at the right time. The *Charmed* sisters learned that hasty love spells lead to reckless results—this seems to be the case in our world as well.

Love spells don't always need to be about finding your soulmate. They can be about finding new friends, discovering new meanings of love in your life, and even self-love. In the meantime, enjoy exploring how love shows itself in your life presently.

KIKI DOMBROWSKI — MARCH 2019

PART I

A LOVE SPELL
INSPIRED BY THE LOVE WITCH

YOU WILL NEED
+ 1 pink candlestick
+ 1 red pillar candle
+ 1 blue pillar candle
+ 1 green pillar candle
+ 1 yellow pillar candle
+ 1 pink long-stem rose
+ Wine or other beverage
+ Paints and brushes
+ Dittany of Crete
+ Juniper berries
+ Pentacle disc
+ Elderflower
+ Rose petals
+ Athame
+ Vervain

STEP 1
This spell is best performed on a Friday between the new moon and the full moon. In preparation for your spell, spend the day painting portraits of the lover you desire and fantasizing about the love you wish to attract.

STEP 2
Gather the herbs listed above and grind them into a fine powder in a mortar and pestle. Dress in a sexy outfit that makes you feel confident and emphasizes your inner love witch!

STEP 3
Prepare your spell's space by anchoring the perimeter with the four pillar candles. Place the green in the north, yellow in the east, red in the south, and blue in the west. Light your candles and sit inside the circle. Bring your athame, chalice, pentacle, herbal blend, pink candle, and rose into the circle with you. Cast a magic circle with your athame. Sprinkle your herbal mixture on the pink candle stick. Take a sip of your libation and hold it to the sky.

Repeat the following words:

Goddess, please send me a beautiful sweet wo/man to love me as I love her/him

STEP 4

Lay in the center of the candles with your arms stretched out above your head and your legs spread apart, so that each of your appendages lays between a set of candles. Chant "love me" over and over, until you feel the Goddess grant your request and flood your body with magnetic attraction to draw your perfect lover near.

STEP 5

In closing, present the rose to the Goddess and thank her for bestowing her gift of love upon you. Take the rose outside and push the stem into the ground so that it stands erect. Pour the remainder of your libation onto the rose and say:

And so this spell is done!

STEP 6

Return inside and hang the portrait of your true love in your home to aid the laws of attraction in drawing them to you.

PART I

TIP

When doing love spells that attract a partner, it is important for you to have a well-rounded idea of who this person is. Spend time meditating and focusing on the different ways this person will affect your life. How will you meet them? How will you add to their life? How will they add to your life? What obstacles stand in your way? What will an average night-in look like? How do they feel about issues that are important to you? What will your lives look like together? Don't be afraid to spend a lot of time letting your brain sift through these questions and others that may arise. It will not only customize your intention fully, but it will also give you perspectives you hadn't considered.

–Tonya A. Brown

NEW MOON SELF-LOVE

The most effective love spell you can perform is one you can perform on yourself. As cheesy as it may be, I have learned from experience that real love starts with self-love. Self-love breathes confidence, and confidence is emotionally sexy. This helps manifest attractiveness.

> An easy approach is to make a mojo bag that you can carry around with you!

YOU WILL NEED
+ Mojo bag
+ Orchid root
+ Rhodochrosite
+ Love-drawing oil blend (equal parts rose, jasmine, sandalwood, and patchouli)

STEP 1
On the new moon, combine the following ingredients in a small pink cloth drawstring pouch: a small tumbled piece of rhodochrosite crystal (the ultimate love stone), an orchid root (clippings are fine, but the entire root is preferred), and 6 drops of a love-drawing oil blend.

STEP 2
While adding the ingredients to the pouch say,

I call on love inside and out, may all negativity and doubt be cast away and out of sight, so that my confidence and self-love take flight.

STEP 3
Pull the drawstrings closed and tie it with six knots—in numerology, this number is associated with love. Leave the pouch on your windowsill overnight to be charged by the new moon! Carry the bag with you or leave on your altar to manifest.

PART II
HERBAL / CRYSTAL SPELLS

PART II

INTRODUCTION A
CRYSTALS OF LOVE GUIDE

The minerals of earth can be utilized in love spells and rituals by creating magical crystal grids, adding to spell bags or pouches, and worn as magical jewelry. When it comes to crystal witch crafting, the below stones are some of my favorites for all acts of love magic.

AMBER promotes confidence, energy, and luck while also being an ample source of magical beauty. It is great to use in glamours and attracting new love.

AMETHYST is a purple quartz variety that is beloved among witches. Known for being a stone of wisdom, amethyst can assist in making wise decisions while in relationships and promotes fidelity in lovers.

CARNELIAN exudes sexuality and confidence. It is great for those wishing to tap into masculine sexual prowess.

EMERALD connects heavily with the heart chakra and can promote emotional healing in love pursuits. It can strengthen relationships and instill faithfulness in partnerships.

GARNET is a stone used to enhance sexual activity.

KUNZITE is a perfect stone for romance and helps lovers to communicate successfully between each other.

HERBAL / CRYSTAL SPELLS

LEPIDOLITE is a self-love stone that helps to instill independence and appreciation for self.

MOONSTONE is a great stone to draw new love into your life. It is also linked to female sexuality.

MORGANITE is a powerful love crystal that amplifies unconditional love. It also represents spiritual love and helps connect you with your divine light.

PINK OPAL helps to reduce trauma and provide renewal through acceptance. It is a stone of peace and tranquility of the heart.

PINK TOURMALINE aids in healing stress and anxiety. It can be used to forge forgiveness in partnerships while promoting security.

RHODOCHROSITE is a gorgeous stone that can sometimes resemble bacon. It assists in helping to find true love, while also healing emotional wounds instilling self-love and self-esteem. It can ease feelings of jadedness and bring you to a state of happiness.

RHODONITE is a lovely mixture of rich pinks and blacks and is known to create and restore balance within the heart. It can help to reduce co-dependency while forging independence in your romantic pursuits so that you do not lose sense of self.

ROSE QUARTZ is the go-to stone for love and compassion, rose quartz has a soft and affection are energy that unlocks the doors to all forms of love.

RUBY is a royal stone of love. It represents wealth and manifestation, making it a great stone to help find new love or strengthen existing partnerships.

PART II

INTRODUCTION B
HERBS OF LOVE GUIDE

The essence of different plants can be added to your love spells and rituals in the form of fresh leaves, powders, incense, and/or essential oils. Each of the plants below are known for their love making abilities and are some of my go-to herbs when it comes to matters of the heart.

APPLE is a classic symbol of wisdom and is often seen as a magical fruit from fairytales. It can be utilized in love magic to find attract new love to you.

CATNIP is known for its triggering happy and mellow feelings within cats. When it comes to love magic, it can be used to attract new love and bring excitement into existing partnerships.

CHILI PEPPER is a spicy herb that can be used in a number of ways. It is generally added to spells for a "quickening" effect, so if you want faster results work with this herb. Its hot qualities can assist in making you appear hot to onlookers and spice up your bedroom life. It also has can be used as a hexing agent in protective magics to cause pain and anguish to those who have caused heartbreak.

CINNAMON is a great herb to use for luck in love and to stimulate sex drives.

DAMIANA is an aphrodisiacal herb known for its power to illicit strong responses in love and lust.

GARDENIA is a beautiful smelling white flower that can add peace and tranquility to love spells.

GINGER can be used when looking for your personal power to grow and attract love with newfound confidence.

HIBISCUS is a delicious herb that is usually found in teas to promote relaxation and sensuality. It can be used in any spells to stimulate sexuality and deep romantic love.

HYACINTH is known for influencing homosexual love.

LAVENDER has the ability to promote calmness and tranquility. Its soothing scent is often used in love spells by breaking down walls of negativity and allowing love to flow freely.

LEMON is a sweet citrus that helps to purify love. It can be used to cleanse negative emotions and open your heart to others.

ORCHID is a beautiful tropical flower. Both root clippings and flower petals can be utilized in attraction spells that promote inner and outer beauty to attract love to you.

ROSE is mother of all love plants. A classical symbol of beauty and love, the rose both opens and protects the heart.

SUGAR CANE is sticky and sweet! Use sugar in love magic to drawn new love to you and help you sweeten the affections of others.

VIOLET is a great herb to use in cooking magic for love. It produces a sweet floral taste that is truly magical. It has also historically been linked to love potions and fragrances as an agent for attracting love.

Discover Self-Love

Ask yourself daily: 'What do I love about myself?' There is no easy solution for becoming completely comfortable in your own skin, or for discovering unwavering confidence. But, the more you care for yourself, the more time you dedicate to your own wellness and joy, the better off you will be.

– Kiki Dombrowski

HERBAL / CRYSTAL SPELLS

CINNAMON FOR LUST

Cinnamon is a great ingredient to add spice to a love potion, rub onto candles, or sprinkle into an incense to heighten the heat in a room. Cinnamon is used to build lust and love so use it creatively to bring a spark into your love life. Be cautious, using too much on skin can be irritating. It is a spice, so go easy. A little goes a long way. For a little unexpected spark, place a cinnamon candy in your mouth just before kissing your love. Ooh la la.

PART II

PASSIONFLOWER IN LOVE MAGIC

Passionflower is said to be a flower helping in attraction work, especially when it comes to attracting friends and allies. Carry passionflower to attract friends and help enhance your popularity.

✶

Consider carrying passionflower in an amulet bag with carnelian, rhodochrosite, and/or rose quartz to attract happy and caring relationships into your life.

✦

You can bathe in passionflower-infused water to attract a potential romantic interest.

☽

Sirona Knight in *Faery Magick* suggests that passionflower can attract more than friends. According to her, you can leave passionflowers at your door to welcome in protective and happy faeries. She also suggests you can tie together passionflowers with pink and red ribbons to attract the one you love into your bedroom.

✶

Passionflower corresponds with the planet Venus. The Venus aspect of the passionflower connects the beautiful plant to goddesses of the heaven: Inanna, Aphrodite, Isis, Bast, Freya, Lakshmi, Venus, Branwen, Astarte, and Ishtar. All of these goddesses connect with beauty, love, sensuality, femininity, and divine creation magick. Venus also links passionflower to female sexuality, marriage, relationships, love, leisure, art, happiness, kindness, and creativity. Consider a blend of Venus essential oils such as rose geranium, gardenia, bergamot with passionflower petals and pure water that has been left out to absorb light from the bright, rising planet of Venus.

HERBAL / CRYSTAL SPELLS

CARDAMOM FOR LOVE

For magical and love purposes of the practical kind, you can add ground cardamom to wine as an aphrodisiac. It can be ground and used as incense to attract love, or you can use whole cardamom pods in love sachets or mojo bags to attract a lover. Store your cardamom sachets in the linen closet, or toss it in the dryer with your bedsheets to diffuse the scent.

Add cardamom to hot chocolate or coffee for an extra lustful kick, and share with someone special. You can add cardamom to many different foods (pies, brownies, etc.) and charge the dish with the magical intention of attracting and promoting love, or for extra invigoration in the bedroom.

The sky is the limit on how creative you can get with this herb. Remember that when it comes to spell work, intention is everything. Whether you decide to add cardamom to an anointed red or pink candle to give your love-inspired candle magic extra herbal oomph, or you plan to bake your beloved a delicious apple pie spiced with cardamom, you really can't go wrong.

JESSICA RIPLEY — FEBRUARY 2018

PART II

LOVE SPELL JAR

Love spell jars are a fun and easy way to draw someone to you. Typically, love spell jars are used to bring in new romantic love or increase self love, but you could just as easily implement the same techniques to bring in new friendships; you only need to switch up the herbs a bit. Jars like this also work well as an offering to love deities and can be a permanent staple on any altars you create for them.

YOU WILL NEED

- Cinnamon or rose incense
- Honey, molasses, or sugar
- A red pen or magical ink
- A jar or bottle with a lid
- Piece of paper that will fit into the jar / bottle

HERBS TO INCLUDE

Basil - harmony
Ginger - passion
Cilantro - marriage
Vanilla - sweetness
Cardamom - loyalty
Lavender - strength in love
Clove - domination, passion
Marigold / Calendula - respect
Rose - love, self-love, romance
Cinnamon - protection, lust, love
Saffron - passion, sexual appetite
Rosemary - protection and fidelity
Sweet orange - joy and sweetness
Jasmine - friendship and purity of heart
Lemon oil - to focus and strengthen the spell
Bay leaves - fertility, healing, and protection
Lemon balm or mint - to send out love signals
Mugwort - to bring dreams of your future love

HERBAL / CRYSTAL SPELLS

STEP 1

Once you have all the items you need, take your pen and piece of paper and write down all the qualities you would like your new love to possess. This can be physical and non-physical qualities; it's up to you. Then, select which herbs you would like to include and grind the herbs together in a mortar and pestle. As you grind the herbs sunwise, visualize this person coming into your life with all the qualities you desire. Burn the paper which contains your qualities and set aside.

STEP 2

Next, burn your chosen incense into the bottle so it fills with the smoke and let the ash gather in the bottle. Once that's done, pour a small amount of honey, molasses, or sugar to your jar. Add your herb mixture to the jar and the ashes of the paper you wrote qualities on, then close it up tight.

STEP 3

Visualise the object of your desire coming to you and end the visualization by saying aloud,

So mote it be.

STEP 4

Keep the bottle with you until the moon begins to wax. Once the moon is waxing, let it sit under a waxing moon and on the day of the full moon, travel to your nearest body of water. The ocean is ideal, but it can also be a stream, creek, or river. Once you're there, say a simple prayer aloud or in your mind as you visualize, then empty the contents into the water to let it free to do its magic.

*If you do not have a body of water near you, then do this instead: on the night of the full moon, make a bonfire and burn the contents of your love spell bottle in the bonfire as you visualize and say any incantations you may select.

PART III

> **TIP**
>
> Everyone knows about bobbing for apples, but this game was originally a matchmaking game. Playing on apples as a symbol of fertility, this old European tradition involves sneakily marking an apple with your name or a special symbol. Available partners "bob" for the apples, and whoever's apple they snag foretells a future match.
>
> –Tianna Sicilia

HERBAL / CRYSTAL SPELLS

APPLES FOR LOVE

Did you know that the apple is one of the rose's closest relatives? This makes this delightful fruit (as well as all parts of the apple tree) a wonderful substitution for roses...well, not always. It might not impress a potential lover to receive a dozen apples, but they can be wonderful in spell work for love and friendship spells. Use sweet apples like honey crisp to bring sweetness and friendship into a relationship, and use tart crisp apples like Granny Smith to bring in a dash of excitement or jazz. Just be sure not to use apples that are too sour or bitter... or the results may be the same.

NATALIE J. WILSON — APRIL 2017

PART II

> ## TIP
>
> Florida Water can amplify emotions and would be an excellent addition to love spells or expressive work. It appears that Florida Water can be added to potions or to amulets to enhance their power. For example, wear Florida Water with a drop of rose essential oil to attract love into your life.
>
> –Kiki Dombrowski

HERBAL / CRYSTAL SPELLS

ROASTING HAZELNUTS

If you plan on burning a bonfire on Samhain night, this is a great game to enjoy. Originally played by the ancient Celts, Scottish women continued this fun game with hazelnuts. Strike up a bonfire, then mark a hazelnut for each of your love interests. Toss them into the fire and whichever burns to ashes instead of popping is said to represent your future betrothed. You may also burn bits of paper or bay leaves with wishes for the New Year written on them, or make offerings such as libations in thanks to your gods and goddesses for a fruitful harvest (metaphorical and literal).

TIANNA SICILIA — OCTOBER 2018

PART II

CRYSTAL GRID FOR SELF-LOVE

YOU WILL NEED
+ 5 pieces of garnet
+ 5 pieces of rose quartz
+ 1 piece of rhodochrosite
+ Photo of yourself (optional)

MANIFESTATION—PASSION / SELF-LOVE

We will tap into rhodochrosite's loving energies and welcome passionate self-love into our lives!

SHAPE—PENTAGRAM

This five-pointed geometric pattern is representative of the four elements and the self. Since this grid calls upon love and stirs up passion, the five-pointed pattern will help concentrate this energy toward us.

FOCUS STONE—1 PIECE OF RHODOCHROSITE

The focus stone sits in the center of the grid. The piece of rhodochrosite will represent the main goal that will be channeled outward through the other stones. Because we are using the pentagram shape, we are ultimately constructing a grid shaped ourselves, with the rhodochrosite positioned perfectly as our heart and core.

WAY STONE—5 PIECES OF GARNET

The way stones will circle the focus stone and help to further amplify the goal represented by the focus stone. Garnet is considered an excellent conduit for passion, desire, sexuality, strength, and courage. In this grid, we will surround our emotional core with a layer of passion. The garnet will represent our blood, full of desire. It is the flaming red that runs through our veins. While it can be utilized for passionate lust in this grid, it can also represent desire on a grander scale, amplifying our heart's pleasures in life.

DESIRE STONE—5 PIECES OF ROSE QUARTZ

The desire stones are the furthest ring of stones in the grid. They fuse the energy from the focus and way stones, helping to manifest the desired goal. Rose quartz is a universal stone for love, beauty, and grace and relates to the awakening of the heart chakra. For this grid, the rose quartz will represent our skin manifesting as external beauty and grace.

MICHAEL HERKES — FEBRUARY 2018

CONSTRUCTION

To build the grid, place the rhodochrosite in the center. Place the five pieces of garnet around it, forming the shape of a star. Above each piece of garnet, place a piece of rose quartz. If you would like, place a picture of yourself under the rhodochrosite to help further manifest the energies in you.

PLACE

This grid should be arranged in a safe place where it will not be disturbed. An ideal location would be a space that you spend a lot of time, since this grid is going to be deeply connected to you. Some examples may be a living room, a home office or den, or perhaps even the bedroom, since it is where many of us spend the most time—outside of work—while sleeping.

ACTIVATE

Once arranged, the crystal grid needs to be activated for use. To activate this grid, you will channel your intent by tracing a pattern over the crystals. Essentially, the pattern is weaving in and out so that each crystal is connected by the intent you are fueling it with.

To do this, I recommend using either an athame or a lit pink or red candle. If neither option works for you, the index finger of your dominant hand will do just fine. Holding your activator over the piece of rhodochrosite, focus your intentions on your heart chakra. Trace a line out and over the top spike in the grid (your head) above the garnet to the rose quartz and back to center. From there, move your activation tool down the spike that would represent your left arm and back to center.

Keep going in a clockwise motion until your legs and right arm are completed. Go around six times (six being the number aligned with love and beauty). While doing this, feel your heart connect with the rhodochrosite. Envision it filling with the overwhelming compassion that radiates from the rhodochrosite in a pink light. Feel it stream into the creative, passionate garnet blood flowing through your veins, pressing up against your luminous rose quartz skin, glowing with radiant beauty.

PART II

ROSE QUARTZ BATH

YOU WILL NEED
- ✦ 2 cups milk
- ✦ Rose quartz
- ✦ Pink candles
- ✦ 6 drops rose oil
- ✦ 3 drops lavender oil
- ✦ 2 tablespoons honey
- ✦ 3 drops ylang-ylang oil

✷

Self-love can be the most comforting and relieving love you can have. It's liberating to develop a caring relationship for yourself before diving into a relationship with someone else. This is a self-love spell for a bath.

☽

Have rose quartz by your bath and light pink candles. Draw a warm bath and blend two cups of milk, 2 tablespoons of honey, 6 drops of rose oil, 3 drops of ylang-ylang oil, and 3 drops of lavender oil in the water.

✷

Stir the water with your hand in a clockwise direction and say the following incantation:

I love myself, I am at peace.

This bath fills me with confidence and love, so mote it be.

☾

Enjoy the relaxing bath and soothing fragrance.

KIKI DOMBROWSKI   OCTOBER 2017

HERBAL / CRYSTAL SPELLS

VIOLETS FOR LOVE

Violets burst forth in color all over lawns in the spring. Pick them and make jellies and teas from them or dry them between the pages of books. They can be used to bring peace and love into your life throughout the year. These little flowers are full of color and happiness. Violets are a symbol of "happy love." They help draw people together in a lasting bond. They strengthen joy and offer prosperity to both romantic loves and friendships alike.

NATALIE J. WILSON — APRIL 2017

PART II

STIMULATE LUSTFUL ENERGY

> Here are two techniques you can use to stimulate lustful energy for your casual encounters.

CRYSTAL GRID

For crystals, you are going to want to stick with garnet, carnelian, and/or red tiger's eye. Each of them brings forth passion, desire, and a flaming heat of sexuality. Try making a crystal grid with these by placing a tumbled garnet in the center of your room (even better if part of your bed falls in the center so that you can conveniently place it under your bed itself), two tumbled carnelians in adjacent corners, and two red tiger's eyes in adjacent corners.

CANDLES

Burning candles is another great way to add lust and sensuality to any room. Of all the elements, fire aligns most with passion and desire. Take a deep-red candle and carve a lust sigil into the wax. There are a variety of different symbols you can use, such as interlocking the planetary symbols of Venus (women) and/or Mars (men) in whatever combination represents you and your desired mate(s). Then anoint your carved candle with a lust oil blend— equal parts musk, patchouli, vanilla, and cinnamon—and roll it in a ground mixture of cinnamon, damiana, ginger, hibiscus, and vanilla bean. While you are dressing your candle, fantasize about your intentions.

HERBAL / CRYSTAL SPELLS

WITCH HAZEL FOR LOVE

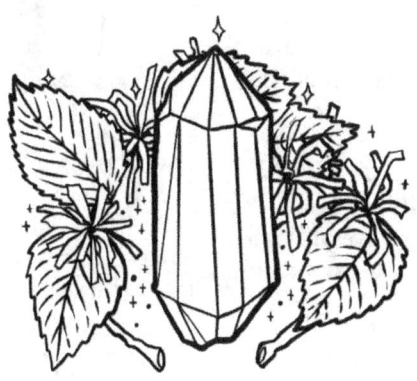

Witch hazel has a long history of being used in love spells. It is believed to be able to heal broken hearts and to help you find love. A witch would simply cut a fresh sprig and carry it on her through the day. When doing a love spell, sprinkle some witch hazel leaves into a lit cauldron for a burning spell of desire and attraction. If casting a spell to improve a relationship that needs healing, wrap a rose quartz with witch hazel leaves and use in your spell.

NATALIE J. WILSON — JULY 2016

PART II

EXERT SEXUAL PRIDE ❖CRYSTAL GRID❖

YOU WILL NEED
- 1 piece of garnet
- 5 pieces of rhodochrisite
- 5 pieces of red tiger's eye
- Photo of yourself (optional)

MANIFESTATION— PRIDE/SEXUALITY
For this crystal grid, we will tap into garnet's sexuality to project pride.

SHAPE— PENTAGRAM
The five-pointed star is the powerful embodiment of self.

FOCUS STONE— 1 PIECE OF GARNET
The garnet will be the focus stone that sits in the center of the grid. It will represent the main goal channeled outward through the other stones.

WAY STONE— 5 PIECES OF RHODOCHROSITE
The way stones will circle the focus stone and help to further amplify the goal represented by the garnet. Rhodochrosite is a loving stone that also helps diminish emotional blockages, helping to restore compassion and self-love. It is also known for its ability to amplify expressive feelings and sexual empowerment.

DESIRE STONE— 5 PIECES OF RED TIGER'S EYE
The desire stones are the furthest ring of stones in the grid. They fuse the energy from the focus and way stones, propelling the energy outward into the universe. Red tiger's eye is known for stimulating kundalini energy, manifesting in sexual passions.

OPTIONAL— A PHOTO OF YOURSELF
As an optional piece, you may wish to place a photo of yourself under the grid, to further help connect the crystals' energies to you.

MICHAEL HERKES · JUNE 2018

CONSTRUCTION

To build the grid, place the garnet in the center. Place the five pieces of rhodochrosite around it, forming a pentagram. From there, you will place a piece of red tiger's eye around each of the rhodochrosite pieces. Instead of placing them on the opposite side of the rhodochrosite, you will place them in the empty pockets made by the rhodochrosite, creating an inverted pentagram with the desire stones. This combination creates an "as above, so below" effect and helps further achieve balance and harmony with your sexual expression.

PLACE

Due to the intention of the grid, it would be best arranged in your bedroom.

ACTIVATE

Once your grid is constructed, it needs to be activated for use. To do so, you will channel your intent by tracing a pattern over the crystals. Essentially, the pattern is a weaving in and out so that each crystal is connected by the intent you are fueling it with. Your activator can be anything you prefer to direct energy from; this can be an athame, a lit candle, an incense stick, a talisman or pendant, a pendulum, or even your index finger. If you have a crystal massage wand or yoni egg, these can also be used.

    Holding your activator over the piece of garnet, focus your intentions on your sexuality and passionate feelings. Ask your crystals to work together to bring forth feelings that support positive sexual expression. Using your activator, begin to trace small circular shapes over the garnet in a clockwise motion. Gradually make the circular shapes bigger and bigger so that it eventually takes up the entire size of the grid. In doing so, begin to feel the negative energy begin to melt away, leaving you able to embrace yourself for who you are.

    When you feel compelled to stop making the circular motions, do so, and trace a pentagram over the rhodochrosite, followed by an inverted pentagram over the red tiger's eye.

    Say, *"As above, so below, my sexuality will ebb and flow."*
Your grid is now activated and ready for use. Enjoy, and remember that all acts of love and pleasure are the goddess's rituals.

PART IV

TIP

Topaz is seen as a major love stone, as it warms the heart. It's warmth sets fire to the vigor of the solar plexus as it merges with the heart chakra, encouraging a wealth of creative energy flow through the heart. Imperial topaz can also help ignite self-assurance and help push one forward during times of doubt. It is a stone that possesses authoritative confidence.

–Michael Herkes

HERBAL / CRYSTAL SPELLS

PET LOVE

Turquoise is a stone of love, satisfying relationships and great friendships. It bestows happiness and fulfillment to the wearer. Turquoise also has incredible protective qualities. It can be used to protect a household, an individual, or even pets. Pet collars with turquoise embossed within are said to protect the animal wearer from harm and theft. Turquoise's powerhouse of physical and spiritual properties is a must have for those seeking clarity, love, and connection.

REBECCA FERREIRA TROY — APRIL 2016

PART II

AMBER FOR ATTRACTION

Amber has been worn to increase attractiveness and enhance self-esteem and a sense of beauty. Anoint amber with a small amount of rose or jasmine oil and carry it with you when you are searching for a romantic partner or going on a date. You can also keep a piece of amber in a love-themed mojo bag. Amber is all about light and growth, so it is not a surprise that it can also be used to manifest abundance and prosperity. If you have a coin jar keep a piece of amber with it, or carry a piece of amber along with your cash. You can also have a piece of amber at your desk if you are trying to bring in more business. Amber has a creative side to it as well. Take a moment to meditate or walk while holding a piece of amber if you are experiencing writer's block or need help attracting inspiration.

HERBAL / CRYSTAL SPELLS

COME AND SEE ME OIL

YOU WILL NEED
- 2 drops ylang-ylang oil
- 8 drops patchouli oil
- 1 drop cinnamon oil
- 6 drops amber oil
- 2-dram bottle

Wear this oil when you are hoping to attract others to you.

☾

Ingredients are meant for 2-dram bottles. Feel free to experiment with amounts if you would like. After adding the ingredients, fill the bottle with a carrier oil like almond oil or jojoba oil.

✳

Before putting on, consider what it is you want to attract into your life, then visualize it clearly and with the most benevolent outcome in your mind.

KIKI DOMBROWSKI — MARCH 2018

PART II

> **TIP**
>
> Garnet is a powerful stone of passion. It helps magnify deep passionate love and intensifies relationships. On that note, garnet is also a highly sexual stone that is known for enhancing and balancing the libido. Wear or carry garnet to attract a mate and place them under your mattress to encourage steamy summer nights!
>
> –Michael Herkes

HERBAL / CRYSTAL SPELLS

STONE FOR VALENTINE'S DAY

There is no better crystal to celebrate Valentine's Day than with rhodochrosite—the ultimate love stone. Found in the Americas, Asia, Africa, and Europe, its name comes from the Greek word *rhodokhros*, meaning rose-colored.

It is most commonly seen in tumbled and sliced form showing incredible bands of color that range from pale pink to deep red, with white and cream-colored ribbons periodically slicing through the colors. Because of this, it can sometimes give off an appearance similar to that of bacon. But that isn't its only form. It can also be found in light-pink crystal rosettes. In rare instances it forms gem-quality crystals in particularly intense shades of red or pink. These rare forms are found in Peru, South Africa, and Colorado and are highly valued.

As a token love stone, rhodochrosite has significant ruling over our emotions, promoting self-love, joy, and personal power. By nurturing these qualities, it creates an abundance of harmony and empathy, while being a powerful stone of attraction. It is capable of bringing new love into your life, both romantically and platonically in the form of deep friendships.

Rhodochrosite is aligned with the element of fire, making it a stone that stirs up passion and energy. In this capacity, it can help in discovering or reawakening talents. It is also seen as a highly transformative stone that helps people overcome stress and deep emotional wounds. It breaks down the walls of grief, pain, shame, stigma, and self-loathing buried deep within. Upon demolishing these walls, it allows us to emerge powerful, fresh, and new, like a phoenix from the ashes. This transformative quality results in confidence and compassion, ultimately cultivating spiritual awakening and ascension to higher states of consciousness.

PART III
DIVINATION

✦

PART III

INTRODUCTION

Divination is the practice of examining events and circumstances beyond present perspectives in an effort to gain insight, wisdom, and answers. Someone who performs divination does so through using psychic abilities, intuitive premonitions, observing omens, and using various tools to gaze beyond their five senses and to tap into the spiritual realm for deeper answers and guidance. In this section we are going to explore various forms of love divination, both traditional and modern, that you can entertain and practice to help with contemplating the powerful topics of love and partnership.

As long as people have sought out the wisdom and knowledge of divination, they have inquired about the topic of love. It makes perfect sense, as our comfort in relationships can make us feel supported, valued, and seen. Romantic relationships and courtship influence moods and life choices, love moves and inspires us, and as the old saying goes: "love makes the world go 'round." One thing that is common about love now, as it was historically, is that love and partnership shape and transform the course of lives. The theme of love will always appear in divination readings because it influences us every single day, in one form or another.

MUNDANE CONSIDERATIONS BEFORE LEAPING INTO LOVE DIVINATION

Anyone who works as a professional divination reader will likely tell you that clients come to them with a variety of questions about love and romance. Clients want to know if relationships are meant to be, if partners are being faithful, what they can do to make a relationship work, or when they can expect to find the right romantic partner. However, there are practical considerations to contemplate before reaching for answers through divination.

USEFUL QUESTIONS TO ASK BEFORE PERFORMING LOVE DIVINATION

+ Is this the right time for you to be in a relationship?
+ Where do you feel you are a great partner and/or friend?
+ Where do you feel you can improve in your partnerships and friendships?
+ Have you determined what your needs are in a relationship?
+ What are indications of a healthy and loving relationship?
+ Are you experiencing red flags in your current relationship?
+ Have you had open and honest communication with the person you are interested in?
+ How would you define self-love and self-care?
+ What have you done to develop a healthy and loving relationship with yourself?
+ Have you really taken the time to ask yourself if you want to know the future of a specific relationship/partnership?

- ✦ Are you willing to do work outside of the divination reading to make a relationship work?
- ✦ How would you react if you heard something you were not expecting or did not want to hear?
- ✦ Are you able to express my feelings truthfully and articulate your needs thoughtfully?
- ✦ Have you meditated on what compromise and collaboration feel and act like in a relationship?

HISTORICAL LOVE DIVINATION: ISSUES WITH GENDER IDENTITY AND SEXUAL PREFERENCES

Traditional love divination was mostly used to help young people see what their marriages would be like and what their romantic suitors would be like. Please note that traditional love divination does have an antiquated feeling to it, in that it did not take into consideration our modern and inclusive views on sexual preferences and gender identity. A majority of folkloric love divination was meant for young women to perform to help them discover their dream man and gaze into their future marriage. We have the opportunity to shift the language into a modernized and neutralized perspective, in a way that all people can feel they can partake in the fun activities of finding love wherever and with whomever they desire. Love is love, and divination can evolve over time just as relationships do.

THE ART OF EMPATHY AND TENDERNESS

Whether you are practicing divination to look for love in your life or in someone else's, be mindful to be gentle and tender when you communicate your interpretations. We all want to have blissful and ever-present love in our lives, and we deserve this. However, the path to deep and lasting love isn't like it is in rom-coms or love songs. It takes effort, communication, loyalty, and trust. There are highs and lows in relationships; moments of devotion and connection, and moments of frustration. The best thing we can do, as readers, is share information as we would like to hear it. There is no need to sugar coat what we see, but we can tread gently when we share information that may be less than blissful.

CREATING A NETWORK OF LOVING RESOURCES

Learning the language of love and how to function in a healthy relationship is not resolved in one divination reading. While traditional divination can be fun to try, and modern forms of divination can deepen insight into patterns of love in your (or your client's) life, it is highly encouraged to seek support and help from multiple resources. Consider seeking out an astrologer who specializes in composite charts for an enriching perspective on a relationship. Consider speaking to a licensed counselor if you need support in working through trauma, self-love issues, love or sex addiction, or couples' therapy. Consider connecting with a life coach who specializes in communication and relationships if you are looking for better ways speak with your partner. Divination can delight and enchant people and offer spiritual guidance, insight and support. However, love, romance, sexuality, and partnership are complex and deserve attention and care so they can grow and evolve in the future.

–Kiki Dombrowski, *Writer*

TRY A DATING SITE
(SAFELY, PLEASE)

WHY NOT? GO FOR IT, HAVE FUN WITH IT. IF ANYTHING, BE OPEN TO ROMANTIC OPPORTUNITIES.

– KIKI DOMBROWSKI

DIVINATION

THREE LUGGIES

There are many varieties of this traditional Scottish divination game, though they all are said to be performed on Halloween night. Three saucers would be placed out in a row. One saucer would have clean water in it, another would have dirty water or milk in it, and another would be left empty. An unmarried person would be blindfolded and asked to put their hand in one of the saucers.

YOU WILL NEED
+ Blindfold
+ 3 Saucers
+ Clean water
+ Dirty water or milk
+ Another person or group

☾

On Halloween night, blindfold the person who wishes to be read.

✷

Place three saucers in a row. Fill one saucer with clean water. Fill the next saucer with dirty water or milk. Leave the final saucer empty. You can randomize the order of the saucers so that the person being read doesn't have any preconceived ideas interfering with their reading.

READINGS
Clean water indicates marrying someone young and pure.
Dirty water indicates marrying someone widowed or unchaste.
An *empty saucer* indicates marriage is not in the future.

PART III

CHOOSE BETWEEN LOVERS

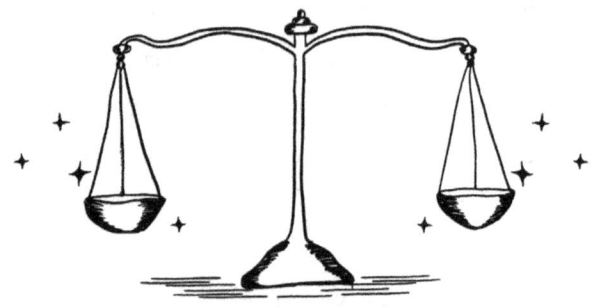

Anthomancy is a divination tool used by hearth, kitchen, and many other witches to help make decisions using flowers as a guide. So how does it work? There is one traditional method to working the flowers and the idea is that you plant one seed per option, label the seeds, and wait to see which grows the healthiest and strongest. The option assigned to that plant will be your answer.

✦

Always be careful when using any type of divination to make choices. Divination only reads our current path, but our path changes constantly with every choice and decision we make. A good rule of thumb is to let divination confirm a decision you've made, instead of letting it make the decision.

TONYA A. BROWN — SEPTEMBER 2016

YOU WILL NEED
+ Flower pots or containers
+ Pen and paper
+ Seeds
+ Water
+ Soil

> Choosing between lovers? Apple seeds can be planted to not only aid in garden magic but aid in love. Brazil nuts aid in affairs of the heart, and cherry can help in both love and aid in divination. You have many options.

STEP 1
Choose seeds or sprouted seeds of a flower that corresponds with the subject of your question.

STEP 2
Choose a good place to keep your plants where they will be safe and grow happily.

STEP 3
Write down the name of your first option on one piece of paper and write your second option's name on another. Fold the papers carefully or place them in separate small envelopes so you will not know which is which.

STEP 4
Plant the seeds and carefully tape each option to a different pot in a way where it will not get wet. Try your best not to know which option is assigned to which pot.

STEP 5
Choose an appropriate amount of time. Let's say I have two months to make this decision, I may want to wait one month to see what the flowers say.

STEP 6
Take care of your plants for that time period. Water, rotate, and make sure each plant gets the equal amount of love.

STEP 7
After a month (or your chosen time period) you can determine which plant grew the healthiest and at that point you can untape your choice from that pot and see what the anthomancy is determining.

PART III

FLOWER DIVINATION

There are many forms of divination that are associated with the plant world. Some of these may be fun for a green witch to try, and others are simply fun to just consider. You've probably done this one before, and it is s a well-known form of flower divination.

✶

Find a patch of daisies and hold
your beloved in your thoughts.

☽

Pick a daisy you are drawn to
and pluck one petal at a time, saying:

They love me, They love me not.

✶

The final petal you end on will reveal to you
if the feelings you have are reciprocated.

Here are several other divination methods using flowers:

FIND A GOOD MATCH WITH BACHELOR'S BUTTONS

Take a bachelor's button and keep it in your pocket when you go on a date. If the suitor is a good match for you, the flower will remain fresh. However, if it is a bad match, the flower will appear shriveled by the end of the night.

CHOOSE BETWEEN LOVERS WITH ROSEBUDS

If you are trying to determine which of two romantic options is best for you, find two roses that look similar and are still closed. Place them in two vases, side by side. Assign one rose to one individual, the other rose to the other individual. The rose that blossoms and looks the most vibrant is the better romantic option for you to pick.

SEE POTENTIAL WITH DANDELION SEEDS

Take a dandelion that is white and all seeds. Think of a person you are romantically interested in. Blow the dandelion seeds. If most of them fly away, it is an auspicious sign for the relationship. However, if many of the seeds still cling to the bud, it is not a good sign.

PART III

> **TIP**
>
> The bright and floral jasmine oil can be used for love, happiness, fertility, and intuition. It is a goddess oil and can be used for love and sensuality spells. It is also said to help raise psychic powers and promote prophetic dreams.
>
> —Kiki Dombrowski

DIVINATION

MOON MAGIC AND PSYCHIC DREAMS

☽ ● ☾

In his book, *The Art of Divination*, Scott Cunningham suggests a mysterious moon divination to try at the full moon. On the new moon, go outside and point a dull-bladed silver knife at the moon.

Say the following incantation:

New moon, true morrow, be true now to me

That I ere the morrow my true love may see.

Speak to no one as you get ready for bed and place the knife under your pillow. Cunningham simply says to then "Remember your dreams." Perhaps this means the dreams will offer images and omens of things to come.

PART III

LOVE IN PALMISTRY

During my dating days, I liked to playfully do simple palmistry as a flirtatious activity to suss out someone's romantic expressions and yearnings. The art of reading palms is complex and enriching, offering meaningful insights into how a person feels and thinks. It can reveal potential and opportunities. However, if you'd like to start exploring the vast world of palmistry, consider looking for a few of these indicators in your partner's palm to discover more about their love language.

FIRE HAND

A person with passion will have a long palm with shorter fingers. This is considered to show a hand ruled by the element of fire. They can have an extravertive streak and be highly energetic. A fire hand reveals charming personality who is turned on by action and adventure. Be mindful that this person can have a temper.

EARTH HAND

A person you can depend on will have a square palm and short fingers. This is considered to show a hand ruled by the element of earth. They can be reliable and supportive, friendly, grounding you and keeping you feeling safe and secure. An earth hand reveals a person who is slow to move in a relationship, but generous and loyal. Be mindful that this person can be stubborn.

AIR HAND

A person who loves communication will have a square palm with love fingers. This is considered to show a hand ruled by the element of air. They can be be thoughtful and inquisitive people, loving to engage in intellectual and detailed conversations. An air hand can indicate a smart and clever person. Be mindful that this person can be fickle.

WATER HAND

A person who is emotional and sensitive has a long palm with long fingers, sometimes with lots of small lines through their palm. This is considered to show a hand ruled by the element of water. They can be tender, sensitive, and emotional. Art and romance are turn-ons. A water hand can indicate a hopeless romantic who loves to dream. Be mindful that this person can become easily jealous.

HEART LINE

The heart line is the thick line that moves across the top of the palm. A line that has a deep curve in it shows someone willing to express their feelings. A straighter line indicates a desire to be more practical in communication. Many fine lines coming off the heart line show a flirtatious streak or a love for the dating life. A deep line shows a deeply emotional person in touch with their feelings. Chains can indicate insecurity.

MOUNT OF VENUS

The Mount of Venus can be found at the base of the thumb. A round and plump Mount of Venus can indicate a pleasure for romance and love, while a flatter one can show someone who is a little less interested in romantic pursuits. If you see a star on the Mount of Venus this indicates an excellent lover.

PART II

TIP

Kiss your love under a bough of mistletoe to ensure that you stay in love forever.

–Em Miiller

DIVINATION

THE PENDULUM

A lot of people use the pendulum for love and relationship enquiries. I recommend that you do not ask questions for which you do not want to know the answers. I advise that for every type of divination.

You can only ask the pendulum yes or no questions. Leave as much potential bias behind you before starting the session. You do not want any bad vibes in your subconscious mind influencing the pendulum and therefore encouraging you to make any decisions you might regret.

When asking questions of the pendulum you should be specific. Use dates, times, places, names, and anything else you can think of which makes the situation as clear as possible.

FOR EXAMPLE

- "Is it a good decision for me to attend the date I was invited to on the 14th of February by David Gosling at the Pizza Place at 7pm?"
- "Is it in [lover's name] and my best interest to ____ on the ___ at ____?"
- "Is it wise for me to trust [lover's name]?"
- "Is it a wise decision to ask [lover's name] to marry me on the ____ at the ____?"

Avoid using words and phrases like "supposed to" or "should." You should also avoid phrases that your higher self can relate to such as "Am I correct in believing that ____?"

Remember to properly calibrate your pendulum before the session to ensure as much accuracy as possible. Pay attention to your emotional state - do not do this after any arguments or tense situations. Do it when you feel at your best; not tired, not emotional, and with no distractions. Ask yourself if it's the right time to ask these questions. Like all rituals in the craft it's vital that you're hydrated, refreshed, clean, and ready to perform.

PART III

FOLK DIVINATION WITH HERBS

Folk divination is used to gain answers to specific questions. Traditionally, the questions revolve around love and marriage, but you can tailor them to your specific needs. You can find specific ways to use folk divination with plants and herbs here:

MULLEIN FOR RECIPROCATED LOVE
There is an old Ozark tradition that involved mullein. A woman would bend a mullein stalk towards her romantic interest's home – if it continued to grow, pointing in the direction of his home, it would indicate that he loved her in return.

LUCKY LOVE LETTUCE
Write the name of a love interest in your garden soil. Plant lettuce seeds in the soil where his/her/their name was written. If the seeds sprout this is a good sign of romantic luck.

YARROW LOVE DREAMS
Harvest a stalk of yarrow under a new moon. Place it under your pillow at before going to bed. If you are to marry, you will have your suitor visit you in your dreams.

ST. JOHN'S WORT ON MIDSUMMER'S EVE
Pick St. John's Wort on Midsummer's Eve. If you wake up in the morning and the flowers still look fresh, you will have good luck with love. Another tradition says to tuck the St. John's Wort flower under your pillow on Midsummer's Eve to dream of your future romantic interest.

DIVINATION

ST. LUKE'S VERSE

YOU WILL NEED
- Wormwood
- Marjoram
- Marigold
- Vinegar
- Thyme
- Honey
- Water

☽

Brew a thimbleful of wormwood, marigold, marjoram, thyme, honey, and vinegar with a half cup of water on St. Luke's Day (October 18th).

Anoint yourself with the concoction at bedtime and say the following:

Saint Luke, Saint Luke,

Be kind to me,

In my dreams let me my true love see

You will then dream of the person you will marry. Some sources say you will see your love interest walking near your bed and he must smile at you for this to be a good sign.

Alternately, you can drink *lavender tea* throught the day. Just Before bed repeat the incantation to dream of your true love.

PART III

LOVE DIVINATION WITH TAROT

If you use tarot, you will find that there are certain cards that indicate love and romance in a variety of ways. Just like palmistry, tarot is a complex and rich form of divination that can offer up a insightful and powerful readings. Two books that focus specifically on love readings in tarot are *Tarot for Love & Relationships* by Elenore Jacobi and *The Tarot Guide to Love and Relationships* by Nancy Shavick – these can be excellent resources if you find you have many clients asking you for readings that focus on relationships. This list represents cards I feel represent different phases or types of love relationships. If I see more than three in any given category, I consider it an indication of patterns or themes in that love reading.

EXPLORING LOVE
The Fool, High Priestess, Hierophant, Lovers,
Strength, The Star, The Moon, multiple Cups cards
Seeing these can indicate it is an excellent time to focus in on what love means and developing emotional skills to build more intimate relationships.

SELF-LOVE
The Fool, Empress, Strength, The Hermit, Temperance, The Star,
World, Two of Swords, Four of Swords, Queen of Swords
Seeing these cards indicates the person getting the reading would benefit from going inwards, and working on the relationship with self.

NEW ROMANTIC OPPORTUNITIES
Ace of Cups, Two of Cups, Lovers
Seeing these cards indicate new romantic opportunities may appear. They are a hopeful sign.

HEALTHY ROMANTIC PARTNERS
Kings and Queens near the Sun Card, Four of Wands, Nine of Cups,
Ten of Cups, Ten of Pentacles, Lovers, Empress and Emperor together
Seeing these cards indicate that relationships being discussed in the reading are healthy and happy.

PLATONIC LOVE
Three of Cups, Four of Cups, Six of Cups, multiple Court cards
These cards indicate that the relationship discussed as a more friendly or familial feel to it, representing a time to focus on friendly social exhanges.

ENDING ROMANTIC OPPORTUNITIES
Three of Swords, Six of Swords, Eight of Cups, Death
Seeing these cards indicate a relationship may be coming to an end or are in a phase of significant transition.

UNHEALTHY ROMANTIC RELATIONSHIPS
The Devil, The Tower, Three of Swords, Five of Swords,
Seven of Swords Nine of Swords, Ten of Swords
Seeing these cards indicates that relationships being discussed are toxic.

PART III

TIP

With the spring also comes the mating season and there is no doubt that carnelian is a master conductor of sexual energy. Its name derives from the Latin word for flesh "carne", also attributed to the lustful word *carnal* which means "pertaining to flesh." Carnelian's vibrant red-orange color aligns it to the Sacral Chakra—responsible for balancing sexuality with a healthy libido. Carnelian is a great stone to wear out on dates and place under your mattress for spring-time frolic and fornication!

–Michael Herkes

DIVINING FIRE

One simple method of divination by fire is scrying. Scrying is divination by gazing, commonly associated with (but not limited to) crystal balls or dark reflective mirrors. Scryers will often gaze into a reflective surface with the intention of seeing divinatory messages. Fire scrying can be a relaxing exercise.

✷

Before you begin, consider what questions you'd like to gain insight into. Rest comfortably by the fire and gaze into its gently glowing embers, allowing your focus to soften. Your vision may even begin going a little blurry.

☽

If your thoughts wander, try and return your attention to your breath and the motion of the fire. You may feel an intuitive answer to your question or see shapes in the embers that contain symbolic messages.

♦

There are different ways to interpret the condition of the flames to divine future events as well. Have a question in mind prior to lighting the fire, and then interpret the way the fire lights and flames move.

✷

It is difficult to find any standard list of flame interpretation, and many sources just contain brief passages on the topic.

Scott Cunningham suggests many flame interpretations in *Earth Power*:
+ It is a good sign if the wood catches on fire and burns quickly.
+ If it is difficult to get a fire going the answer is not as optimistic for the moment and needs to be returned to at a later time.
+ Love and romance are omens if the fire moves to one side of the fire pit.
+ Difficulties and challenges will follow if the fire crackles frequently.
+ There is important news ahead if sparks fly into the air.

PART III

APPLES AND SAMHAIN

Apples hold a special place in Celtic mythology, where they are connected to otherworldly magic and considered to be the fruit of the dead, and a symbol of magic, beauty, and immortality. The Celtic god Dagda lived in a kingdom with always-fruited and abundant apple trees.

Apples are harvested in the fall and were likely a staple item in Samhain feasts. They've played an important role in the food, games, and fortune telling of Halloween, thus making them a key ingredient in celebrations.

Over time, many forms of fortune telling involving apples became fun party games. Bobbing for apples was originally a marriage divination: the first person to bite into the apple would be the first person to marry in the upcoming year.

Although there is no concrete evidence, bobbing for apples may actually have its roots dating all the way back to Celtic times. There is evidence however, that it was in practice during medieval times. Manuscript illustrations from as early as the 1300s show servants bobbing for apples.

Apples are said to have the magical powers of enhancing beauty, assisting in healing, and being a special addition to a love spell. Samhain is an excellent time to work with dreams. Taking note of images and messages from dreams can bring insight into waking life.

※

On Samhain take an apple and slice it in half, horizontally. Carve a topic you wish to know the future about in the flesh – for example, money, health, or love. Anoint the apple with one drop of sandalwood oil, one drop of jasmine oil.

☽

Hold the apple back together in your hands and recite the following:

May this apple bring to me dreams of prophecy.
This Samhain give me dreams with fortune's view,
Allow me to see the future true.

※

Place the apple by your bedside and see if your Samhain dreams hold any messages about the future.

CELEBRATE LOVE TAROT SPREAD

Use this tarot spread when working on love magic or when you would like to examine how love is playing a role in your life. This is especially fun to work on or near Valentine's Day, Beltane, Litha, or at wedding celebrations.

Card 1: In what part of your life you need to show the most love
Card 2: How you can go about expressing love more clearly to yourself and others
Card 3: The most important lesson of love for this time in your life
Card 4: What hobby or talent you need to show more love to
Card 5: What people love most about you
Card 6: How you show love to a partner
Card 7: What you need to work on most in terms of loving people in your life
Card 8: Future events that will affect your love life

DIVINATION

OMENS OF WEATHER

Many witches enjoy the magical and spiritual feeling of a bright full moon, but the moon can also give us omens and help us with our divination. Selenomancy is the divination of the appearance and the phases of the moon. While you are outdoors celebrating the moon's magic, consider using it in your next divination practice!

There are plenty of omens about the weather based on the moon. If weather omens are of interest to you, consider getting an annual copy of *The Farmer's Almanac*. It is a great source for folklore predictions about weather, the moon, and astrology.

WEATHER PREDICTIONS BASED ON THE MOON

- ✦ A red ring around the moon means someone has fallen in love.
- ✦ An old Welsh tradition told women to look at the first full moon of the New Year through a silk handkerchief. The number of moons she'd see through the silk veil would reveal the number of months she'd remain unmarried.
- ✦ It is lucky to move during a new moon and believed abundance will come into the home as the moon grows fuller.
- ✦ A full moon that occurs on a Monday is considered lucky. In the south of France a new moon that occurs on Friday is considered unlucky.
- ✦ Rainy and windy weather will follow after a new moon on a Saturday.
- ✦ If the moon looks pale, rain will follow.
- ✦ When the "horns" of the crescent moon look sharp, it'll rain the next day, or if it is winter there will be frost.

PART III

CANDY HEART DIVINATION

Like a fortune cookie, conversation candy hearts come with a message and therefore can be incorporated into divination. Though they are not a traditional divination tool, they do make for a great alternative. They are also a really great resource for the love witch on the go, as they are easily obtained from grocery stores and pharmacies in February and March!

✷

To use, simply obtain a bag or box of conversation hearts and focus your intent on what you need insight on. If you do not have a specific question, try asking the universe to show you what it is you need to know right now in this moment. Close your eyes, reach in the bag, and pull out the heart you connect most with. Pull it out and reflect on what the statement says.

☽

Depending on the brand of conversation hearts you get, there may be different sayings. On the neighboring page there are some of my interpretations for commonly used phrases today. If you pull one that is not listed here, use your intuition and think about how the phrase reflects best to your question. You can also pull multiple ones and determine what each position would mean, similar to tarot!

DIVINATION

CANDY HEART KEY

- *Call Me* – This suggests communication is necessary. If you are holding onto something, it's best to speak clearly (from the heart).

- *Cutie Pie* – This answer relates to appearances. Remain cognizant of your physical demeanor and overall persona in the public eye.

- *Hug Me* – Hugs provide comfort in a time of need. This phrase may represent sadness or that healing is necessary.

- *I Love You* – Someone has romantic feelings for you. If asking a yes or no question, this definitely signifies yes!

- *Kiss Me* – Aligned with the water element and denotes emotion, wisdom, healing, and intuition.

- *LOL* – Lots of laughs is a sign of the trickster. Beware! All is not what it seems.

- *Love Bug* – Aligned to the air element and denotes intellect, thought, communication, and socialization.

- *Only You* – This response suggests solitude and taking time for introspection.

- *Love Me* – This relates to self-love and self-care. Receiving this heart suggests taking a moment to do what you love and to spend some time indulging in what makes you happy.

- *No (anything)* – Anything containing the word "no" should be a sign of caution. If you asked a yes or no question, this signifies that you should not move forward.

- *Red Hot* – Aligned to the fire element and denotes passion, confidence, courage, and excitement.

- *Soul Mate* – A sign of divine love. Your ancestors, god/desses, and/or spirit guides are watching over you with support.

- *True Love* – To receive this message is to understand that you are currently on the right path and encourages you to continue.

- *XOXO* – An encouragement to be flirtatious.

- *You Rock* – Aligned to the earth element and denotes foundation, grounding, material objects, and prosperity.

PART IV

> **TIP**
>
> Rose oil is used for love, lust, sensuality, beauty, and gentleness. Add a few drops of this essential oil to a bath for self-love and self-compassion.
>
> —Kiki Dombrowski

DIVINATION

TWO LOVERS TRIANGLE SPREAD

This is a reading for deciding between two potential romantic interests.

STEP 1
Place The Lovers card at the top of the spread.

STEP 2
Pull one royalty card of your choice to represent *Partner Option 1*.

STEP 3
Pull another royalty card of your choice to represent *Partner Option 2*.

STEP 4
When you are ready, lay out your cards.

Card 1: Positive aspects of a relationship with Option 1
Card 2: Challenging aspects of a relationship with Option 1
Card 3: How Option 1 feels about you
Card 4: How you and Option 1 operate together
Card 5: Outcome/answer/solution card for potential in a relationship with Option 1
Card 6: Positive aspects of a relationship with Option 2
Card 7: Challenging aspects of a relationship with Option 2
Card 8: How Option 2 feels about you
Card 9: How you and Option 2 operate together
Card 10: Outcome/answer/solution card for potential in a relationship with Option 2

PART III

LOVE INSIGHT

> This is a card-reading spread that will help you gain insight into a relationship.

WHEN
Divination can be done on any day. However, Monday is considered the moon's day—the moon is typically associated with divination—and if you like the idea of organizing your spell work this way, Monday is a good day.

WHERE
This spell should be done wherever you meditate best because meditation is one way to connect to the spirit realm, where messages are passed along.

STEP 1
Set up your space with your cards and other items you enjoy having around when you read, such as candles or incense. Make sure you are undisturbed and in a place where you can meditate.

STEP 2
Close your eyes and meditate, letting your mind reach a higher state of consciousness.

STEP 3
Once you are ready, lay out your cards.

Card 1: Current state of the relationship
Card 2: How the outside world views the relationship
Card 3: The querent's mindset regarding the relationship
Card 4: The partner's mindset regarding the relationship
Card 5: How the querent adds to the partner's life
Card 6: How the partner adds to the querent's life
Card 7: How the querent fears the relationship can go wrong
Card 8: How the partner fears the relationship can go wrong
Card 9: Where this relationship will end up on its current trajectory

DIVINATION

MIRRORS

Mirrors are thought in some traditions to be the windows of the soul, adding the Uruz rune—for strength, health, changes, and passage—to a mirror, could be a wonderful way to set an intention (for instance: I am going to love myself more), and stick to it. With the help of your chosen Rune, every time you view yourself, you will be filled with compassion and unconditional love for the person staring back at you—which is your lovely self!

PART III

LOVE DIVINATION CRYSTAL KIT

YOU WILL NEED
Small pink bag
Rhodochrosite
Rose quartz
Unakite
Garnet
Jet
Citrine
Howlite
Sodalite
Amethyst
Crystal quartz
Small green bag

> Lithomancy is the divination of crystals. This divination kit is for the purpose of focusing on love. It can be used when interested in examining an important relationship.

STEP 1
Keep one of each of the following crystals in the pink bag: rhodochrosite, rose quartz, unakite, and garnet. Keep one of each of the following crystals in the green bag: jet, citrine, howlite, sodalite, amethyst, and crystal quartz.

STEP 2
The crystals in the pink bag represent the potential love interest. Pull a crystal from the bag or lay them out in front of you. With your eyes closed, move your hand over each of the crystal. Select the one you feel most drawn to. If you have a certain person in mind you can also select the crystal that best represents who you have in mind.

RHODOCHROSITE
Rhodochrosite represents a relationship with yourself and indicates being in a solitary period where you turn the attention to self-love and self-care.

ROSE QUARTZ
Rose quartz represents an emotional relationship that has a deeper emotional connection.

UNAKITE
Unakite represents a relationship that is platonic. In other words, this is indicates a relationship that is best in a friendly form.

GARNET
Garnet represents a physical relationship that is lustful and sexual in nature.

KIKI DOMBROWSKI

DIVINATION

STEP 3
Next, the crystals in the green bag will give you the message/interpretation to go alongside the love interest crystal. Pull a crystal from the bag or lay them out in front of you. Close your eyes, and select the one you are most drawn to.

JET
Jet represents pauses, challenges, and/or transitions. It can also be the answer "no." Jet with garnet represents a passionate tryst that is short lived and likely toxic. Jet with Rose Quartz shows a challenging time with a romantic partner and a need to pause before reacting. Jet with Unakite shows a disagreement with a friend or family member – it is a difficult relationship that needs space and time. Jet with Rhodochrosite reveals a time to focus on helping yourself as you move through transitions or work through trauma.

CITRINE
Citrine represents manifestation, happiness, fun, and success. It can also be the answer "yes." Citrine with garnet suggests that the current wild relationship is all about pleasure and learning about what turns you on. Citrine with rose quartz can indicate marriage, children, life events with a happy relationship. Citrine with unakite can indicate celebrations, parties, social events to connect with friends and family. Citrine with rhodochrosite represents a phase of self-discovery that leads to better understanding what makes you feel your best.

HOWLITE
Howlite represents potential and slow momentum. It can also be the answer "maybe." Howlite with garnet represents a relationship that would benefit from slowing down. Howlite with rose quartz represents a long-term relationship that is starting to blossom – do not lose hope. Howlite with Unakite shows a gentle, low maintenance friendship and can indicate there is an opportunity to step up and be a supportive friend. Howlite with Rhodochrosite indicates learning how to bring comfort and quiet into your own life.

SODALITE

Sodalite represents healing and support. It indicates a focus on healing, balance, and peacefulness. Sodalite with garnet reminds you that you can explore your sexuality without shame, but instead celebrate knowing what brings you pleasure. Sodalite with rose quartz suggests that there are emotional healing opportunities and peaceful moments of balance with your romantic interest. Sodalite with unakite indicates a time to have intimate gatherings with friends and help friends heal. Sodalite with rhodochrosite indicates a time to take care of your health and energy.

AMETHYST

Amethyst represents a soulful connection and a feeling of being deeply connected to someone. It indicates spiritual development and meaningful lessons through this relationship. Amethyst with garnet suggests that you feel a magnetic pull to someone, but that there is no long-term loyalty from this interaction. Amethyst with rose quartz indicates a soulful, long term relationship where you learn about authentic love. Amethyst with unakite indicates a powerful and inspiring friendship and someone you have been friends with for more than one lifetime! Amethyst with rhodochrosite shows that there is an opportunity to learn self-love through spiritual practices.

CRYSTAL QUARTZ

Crystal quartz represents communication and honesty. It indicates a focus on speaking your truth, being forthcoming with your intentions, and using language to understand yourself and the other person. Crystal quartz with garnet suggests that you tell someone you are attracted to you how you feel or to explore flirtation. Crystal quartz with rose quartz indicates an opportunity to really discuss emotional concerns and create mutual goals. Crystal quartz with unakite suggests that it is time to reconnect with friends through communication. Crystal quartz with rhodochrosite suggests that a letter to yourself, journal, and/or remember to practice loving and forgiving communication with yourself.

DIVINATION

PULL THE STALK

Kale stalks or cabbage were used for love divination. Traditionally, a young person would be sent out into a garden at night, usually at Halloween. The young person would pull a kale stalk or cabbage, and it would be examined to determine the features of his/her/their future mate.

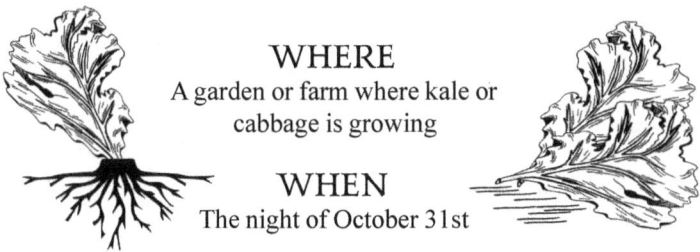

WHERE
A garden or farm where kale or cabbage is growing

WHEN
The night of October 31st

READINGS
After pulling the stalk from the ground, the readings are very literal.

☽

If a lot of dirt clings to the vegetable it is a sign of wealth, while no dirt is a sign of poverty, and some dirt is a sign of modest means.

✶

If the vegetable is sickly, it can indicate that the partner would have poor health, or it would be a poor match.

☾

A short and stunted stalk can indicate physical characteristics of a mate or attributes of the relationship. This is also true for a tall and healthy stalk, which could suggest a tall, healthy partner or relationship.

✶

The disposition of a partner is thought to be ascertained through the plant's flavor (sweet, bitter, bland, flavorful, strong, etc).

PART IV
KITCHEN WITCH SPELLS

PART IV

INTRODUCTION

The act of cooking is magical: we take the bounty of the world around us and transform it into sustenance that gives us nutrition, energy, and health. Cooking is an inspired act that allows cooks, chefs, and bakers to not only create sustenance, but to also create a work of art that delights and awakens the senses. Think about your long-term relationship with the kitchen: what cake did you have for your birthday every year as a child? What favorite dish do your friends ask you to make every year for a winter dinner party? Which herbs do you feel power from when you handle them? How do you feel when you freshly stock your cupboards? The kitchen is a palpable magic, and because of that, it is only natural that there are witches who are drawn to bringing the craft into their kitchen.

KITCHEN WITCH SPELLS

Kitchen witches wield the power of the earth. Taking plants, oils, ingredients, and using them to concoct potions, charms, and meals. Whether it is an oil to dress your candles during a spell, a charm bag to carry with you while you are on a date, or a loving meal you make so someone who eats it can feel your love within them, knowing the power of plants and what they can accomplish magically is a valued and honored skill. Kitchen witches can use their ability to feel the magical properties of food and dishes for powerful love magic. With a dash of basil and a clockwise turn of a wooden cooking spoon, a simple pasta meal can turn into an affectionate feast meant to bring nurturing comfort to its diners.

Food has always had an enchanting power over people, and through the ages, we have learned to use food to conjure love and romance. There is an old saying that you can win a man's (or woman's) heart through their stomach, implying that food can make someone fall in love with you. And, there is also a saying that says the kitchen is the heart of the home. The Ancient Romans and Greeks believed oysters where aphrodisiacs that awakened sensual emotions, and today we equate strawberries and champagne with romantic date nights.

In this chapter we are going to explore love spells in kitchen witchcraft. Remember that love spells in the kitchen do not need to be limited to aphrodisiac dishes that titillate a partner. Kitchen work encompasses all plant uses within magic – be it a meal, an oil steeped for a week for your ritual bath, or a carefully crafted charm bag while sitting surrounded by all the herbs you own at your kitchen table. When it comes to herbs, plants, food, and the kitchen – all magic can be obtained there.

–Kiki Dombrowski and Tonya A. Brown

Make your romantic partner a priority

If you are in a relationship, give it special attention this year. Are the two of you still making time to go on dates? What do you do together that is just for the two of you? Do you still flirt? Having a romantic relationship takes patience, communication, and maintenance. Give it priority.

– Kiki Dombrowski

KITCHEN WITCH SPELLS

ᘛALLUREᘚ THROUGH TASTE

It has been said before that a way to a person's heart is really through their stomach! The next sense to highlight is the taste buds. Certain foods promote sexual response, called aphrodisiacs. In this stage, you are going to fuse together a bit of kitchen witchery with lusty glamour by making a dinner that promotes aphrodisiacs.

So what's on the menu? For the meat eating witches out there, high protein meats (particularly red meat) stimulate chemicals within our bodies that create excitement and accelerate our heart beat. Other foods known for their aphrodisiacal qualities are oysters, truffles, asparagus, chocolate, red wine, champagne, figs, strawberries, etc. With that in mind, a sample dinner menu may include a first course of oysters, a main course of steak with truffle sauce and asparagus, and a dessert with fresh luscious strawberries, chocolate, and whipped cream. If you are unable to cook a meal, dining out is always a good option. Do a bit of research on different types of aphrodisiacs and select a restaurant or items from the menu that whet the passion food appetite.

PART IV

HOW TO CREATE A LOVING MEAL

Love goddesses are perfect to ask for help during the month of love to help heal broken hearts, mend relationships on the outs, look for a new love interest or stir the embers up in a current relationship. Candle spells, offering of flowers and honey will get their attention and hopefully help with your petition!

It is always nice to do something special for your significant other but when Valentine's Day comes around we make an extra effort to show them how much they mean to us! When cooking for your lover, focus those happy feelings into the meal as you would any spell work. When preparing several courses you can charge each dish with a different intent from a tease, to the buildup and climax! Have fun and try different things to see how your lover responds.

Cooking with your partner can be a sensual experience that might encounter some, ahem, interruptions! Go with the flow, enjoy it and make some great food together or just skip straight to dessert!
We have all heard of the aphrodisiac. Foods that stimulate and encourage desire, stamina, sensitivity, and the like. Science and the body's physiology are major factors when considering how well an aphrodisiac works or what its use may be.

✳

Chilis are a stimulant that increase blood flow, aiding erections and clitoral engorging. Antioxidants such as pomegranates, raspberries, blueberries, and blackberries do the same. Herbs and spices such as cinnamon, clove, oregano, cumin, bail, ginger, garlic, thyme, and cilantro also increase blood flow.

☾

Wine, an antioxidant, and alcoholic spirits are known to help a person relax but too much can have an adverse effect like sleepiness so watch your consumption and opt to use it in your cooking instead for some added flavor.

✳

Foods that produce serotonin can also be classified as an aphrodisiac. Serotonin is a chemical in the body that stabilizes our mood and gives us the sensation of feeling good leaving you receptive to your partner and more inclined to "be in the mood." Almonds, pumpkin seeds, sesame seeds, tomatoes, avocados, pineapple, mango, and bananas are some examples. Chocolate, especially dark, also develops serotonin so don't feel bad about having some, it literally makes you feel good.

☽

Honey promotes the development of testosterone. The mineral boron is found in honey aides the use of estrogen in women. Honey can increase the level of nitric acid in the body, which is a chemical released into the blood during arousal. It can be used as a sugar substitute in many recipes and sometimes found in savory ones such as barbeque sauces and used to compliment tart flavors. Drizzle some over berries on your partner for a sweet treat!

♦

Outside of all the science, it's important to know your partner. What are the foods or smells that have them hovering into the kitchen to lay a gentle kiss on your neck or cheek? What makes them say "yum" or close their eyes when taking a bite? Use that as inspiration for a fantastic meal.

PART IV

TIP

Make a fruit-flavored lip balm to give your lips a soft, smooth touch. Add half a teaspoon of coconut butter and half a teaspoon of rapeseed or olive oil in a bowl. Add a drop or two of strawberry essential oil and mix together.

–Emma Kathryn

PASSION CHARM

To add passion to a current relationship add all of the elements below into a pouch and tuck into your nightstand. Leave the pouch there as long as possible. Recharge and cleanse monthly by leaving it on your windowsill during full moons.

YOU WILL NEED
- 2 parts Adam and Eve root
- 1 dehydrated apple peel
- 1 part cayenne pepper
- 3 parts rose petals
- 2 parts cinnamon
- Pouch (red is ideal)

PART IV

DIY PASSION CANDLES

YOU WILL NEED

- Pan
- Water
- Hibiscus
- Myrtle leaf
- Tea candles
- Cinnamon oil
- Red rose petals
- Ylang-ylang oil
- Pieces of red wax (candle or sealing)
- Rosemary (oil or herb)
- Any other oils or herbs you deem appropriate for you and your partner.

I created these little passion candles over a year ago when I was dating someone who was perfect on paper... but we lacked any passion. While these candles worked, and provided passion when lit, they did not solve the underlying problem. He simply wasn't right for me. As with any love or passion spell, sometimes it can be more exhausting than it's worth to create something that was never there to begin with. I recommend using these for a relationship that has already proven to have spark, but may be in a rut. Enjoy these with a partner to aid in a date night, surprise rendezvous, or for a cuddly night on the couch.

STEP 1

Place the tea candles into your pan and fill with just enough water to fill halfway up the candle. DO NOT let the water touch the wax. Turn your stove on low and let the candles melt in their tins as you prepare the other ingredients.

STEP 2

Once you have assembled all of your ingredients carefully add them to your candles. Use a toothpick to help keep the wick in place and to keep the ingredients in. Add the following to each candle: 3 drops ylang-ylang, 2 drops cinnamon, 1 drop (or sprinkle of herb) rosemary, piece of hibiscus, a sprinkle of crushed rose petals, and a sprinkle of myrtle leaf. Feel free to grind up the herbs together beforehand, but put the oils in directly on their own. Add in other herbs and oils that your chose. Wax may overflow out but this is OK.

STEP 3

Turn off the stove. As your candles begin to cool and solidify push a piece of red wax into them. This will represent your hearts as one. Let cool for at least an hour or two before removing from water and storing. Light and use when needed.

LOVE SPELL COOKIES

Love spell cookies are a fast and easy way to get people to warm to you, to increase self-love and contentment, or to give new love a little push.

These cookies may be left out under the full moon or passed through rose or cinnamon incense to charge. They work well as an offering to love deities such as Eros, Aphrodite, Venus, or Freya. These are also a great way to celebrate any love-related holidays like Beltane, Lupercalia, or even Valentine's Day. Whatever your reason, these cookies are delicious and guaranteed to put anyone who tries them in a great mood!

COOKIE INGREDIENTS

+ 2 sticks butter, softened
+ 1 cup sugar
+ 1 egg
+ 1½ teaspoons baking powder
+ 2½ - 3 cups flour
+ 1 teaspoon vanilla extract
+ 2 - 3 teaspoons cinnamon
☾ Optional: pinch of cardamom, 1 tablespoon food-grade rose petals (ground up)

ICING INGREDIENTS

+ 2 cups powdered sugar
+ 1 - 2 tablespoons pasteurized egg whites
+ 1 - 3 teaspoons milk
+ 2 teaspoons cream of tartar

RECIPE

1. Preheat oven to 350° F.
2. Sift flour, sugar, baking powder, and cinnamon.
3. Slowly work the butter, egg and vanilla into the flour mixture.
4. Roll dough out with a rolling pin, about ¼ inch thick, between two pieces of parchment paper.
5. Cut out dough into circles or hearts as desired, and lay on a baking sheet.
6. Put the baking sheet in the freezer for 10-30 minutes.
7. Bake for 10-12 minutes, then let cool.
8. Combine icing ingredients and apply to cookies.
9. Enjoy!

TIANNA SICILIA

PART IV

LUSTCRAFT POTION

Smell is so important because it naturally tells us when something is not good for us. The smell of rotten food triggers a response in our brain that the food is spoiled and no longer nutritious. The human body creates smells that both attract and repel as well. Some of these smells are pheromones that naturally make us more attractive and initiate sexual response from others.

With glamour magic, we can enhance our pheromones to increase attractiveness through essential oils. Essential oils are oils that are made from fragrances extracted from a plant or other source. For this sense, you will make a lust potion to wear for the evening. My simple lustcraft oil blend recipe calls for three fragrances that are known for the love and lust notes.

YOU WILL NEED
- Black pepper oil* (may substitute black pepper with cinnamon or patchouli oil)
- Musk oil
- Rose oil
- Vial

RECIPE

Mix equal parts of rose, black pepper, and musk oils in a small vial. This blend is a well-balanced unisex blend that stimulates intense attraction regardless of sex. However, if you are after a more feminine scent, add more rose. For a more masculine scent, increase the black pepper.
*Note: black pepper can irritate the skin. Try putting a small drop on your skin prior mixing the oil to test for irritation. If you are unable to use black pepper, cinnamon or patchouli oil are good substitutes.

Roses
Roses are a symbol of love, beauty, and elegance. This smell awakens our senses with a burst of lush florals which intensifies with an explosion of spice from the black pepper.

Black Pepper
Black pepper and other spicy herbs are known for their ability to accelerate the heart rate and create excitement.

Musk
The mixture is topped off with a bit of musk. Musk is an animal pheromone that used to be collected from their glandular secretions. Today, it is created synthetically and regularly used in perfumes/colognes and essential oil blends for allure. Dab your lustcraft potion behind your ears, your wrists and your clavicle/chest region and get ready to really attract some attention!

PART IV

SIMPLE LOVE POTION

YOU WILL NEED
- 3 drops jasmine or rose geranium absolute
- 12 drops ylang-ylang essential oil
- 1 ounce bleeding heart essence
- 4 ounces distilled rosewater
- 1 ounce carnation essence
- 5 ounces brandy or vodka

✸

Combine all of the ingredients together into a glass bottle.

☾

Charge it under a waxing moon.

✸

Wear as a perfume splash or use it in spell work.

KITCHEN WITCH SPELLS

BLUE MOON INCENSE

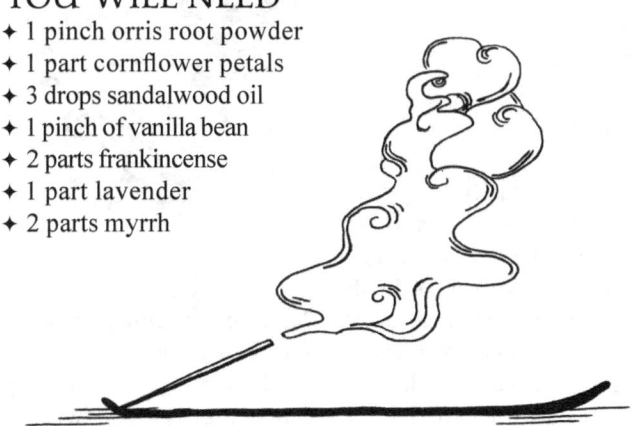

YOU WILL NEED
+ 1 pinch orris root powder
+ 1 part cornflower petals
+ 3 drops sandalwood oil
+ 1 pinch of vanilla bean
+ 2 parts frankincense
+ 1 part lavender
+ 2 parts myrrh

☽ ✶ ☾

Blend all the ingredients well and burn a pinch at a time over a charcoal briquette. White sandalwood powder would be excellent for this blend; however, it is not as readily available as red sandalwood powder. As a substitute, you can add a drop of sandalwood essential oil. Burn this incense for blue moon rituals, gaining truth or clarity into a situation, smudging divination tools, love spells, or fertility spells.

KIKI DOMBROWSKI — MARCH 2018

PART IV

PROTECT LOVE CHARM

YOU WILL NEED
- Small jar or vial with lid
- Moon water
- Dried sage
- Cinnamon
- Palo santo
- Rosemary
- Cloves
- Honey

CLEANSE
Rinse vessel out with moon water if you have it, or direct some sage smoke into the vessel to finish the cleansing. Set that in a sunny window to dry while you prepare the rest. Do the same with your other ingredients (except the honey). Light the palo santo for blessing as you work. You do not need an invocation for this to come to fruition. You simply need to remain present and be thoughtful about your actions while you work. Likewise, the quantities of each ingredient can vary. Use your intuition to guide you. Perhaps you want more emotional connection; in which case, add extra cloves. Maybe you want to spice things us a bit; in that case, it's cinnamon you want.

IMBUE
Put the charm either outside or in a window on the new moon. This is, of course, after you've spent some quality time with your charm, allowing your intent to pour into it. I'd suggest leaving it there for three days.

PLACE
Keep it someplace safe within your bedroom. A nightstand is ideal.

MAINTAIN
It's a good idea to recharge your charm from time to time. Monthly, yearly, quarterly, base this off of what you feel in your gut.

MICHELLE DENISON — FEBRUARY 2017

KITCHEN WITCH SPELLS

FAIRY WINE

YOU WILL NEED
- 2 cups of milk (of your preference)
- 1 teaspoon of dried lavender buds
- 1 teaspoon of dried rose petals
- 1 tablespoon of honey

Fairy Wine is said to aid in fertility during rituals and is also a great option for offerings to the Fae.

✷

Heat the milk up in a saucepan and once you start to see steam add in the herbs and honey.

☾

Allow the mixture to warm steadily, but try to prevent boiling or simmering.

✷

After about 10 minutes strain and serve.

☾

If you plan to make this in advance, store without straining. When you are ready to serve, reheat in a saucepan and then strain at that time.

TONYA A. BROWN — MAY 2017

PART IV

> **TIP**
>
> Cranberry is a water element, associated with the planet Mars. These berries are associated with fall/winter altars and are used in love and protection spells. Use cranberry juice in spells as an alternative to red wine.
>
> –Amelia Ferrari

KITCHEN WITCH SPELLS

ROSY LOVE OIL FOR JUNE

YOU WILL NEED
- 2-dram oil bottle
- 6 drops rose oil
- 3 drops vanilla oil
- 1 drop patchouli oil
- 9 drops frangipani oil
- 1 drop ylang-ylang oil
- 6 drops dragon's blood
- Carrier oil of your choice
- Dried rose petals*
- Rose quartz*

*optonal

Love is in the air in June! June is named after Juno, the goddess who rules over marriage. During the month of June, blend together this oil to attract love into your life.

STEP 1
In a 2 dram oil bottle mix oils listed above.

STEP 2
If you would like, add one or two dried rose petals or a piece of rose quartz, though this is optional. Fill the remainder of the bottle with a carrier oil of your choice and blend.

STEP 3
Before putting it on, hold the bottle and visualize what it is you would like to attract into your life.

KIKI DOMBROWSKI

PART IV

UNITING WITH WINE RITUAL

A wine ritual is the use of wine to symbolize the uniting of two people. A typical ceremony includes a glass of red wine and a glass of white wine, both representing different aspects of your union, for example the robustness and the purity of your love. They can also represent the differences between you and your partner, for example your boldness and their sweetness. Red and white wine are most commonly used because they are visually different which adds to the symbolism. The two wines are then poured into a new glass to symbolize the unity of your marriage through the mixing of the wines. Once the two wines are poured into the same glass you can no longer separate them just as you would no longer be able to part the couple being married. These rituals are completely customizable. You do not have to use red and white wine, you can use white and white or red and red or whatever you want. The goal is to choose whatever you feel best captures your marriage. Some wine ceremonies don't even blend wines but instead have the couple share a single cup of wine that has the same symbolic meaning.

SAMPLE WINE RITUAL

A good wine, like a good marriage, is the result of many years of hard work, nurturing, and commitment. (Name) and (name) have spent many years cultivating their love for each other. On this table there are two good glasses of wine. One red and one white. The red wine represents their passion and robustness. The white wine represents the purity and lightness of their love.

Together they will blend these wines as they are blending their families. Creating a new wine altogether. One that is bitter as it is sweet. But this new wine cannot be unmade just as this union cannot be unmade. (name) and (name)'s marriage will continue to grow stronger with age and become more rich and complex just as a fine aged wine.

[Blend the wines]

They will now drink to their union. May they never thirst.
So whether you are getting married or not, here's to wine, a great uniter. A uniter of covens, friends, families, and sometimes even enemies. May you never thirst. May your wine glass always be filled with good wine. May you always drink it with good friends

PART IV

EROTIC ÉCLAIRS

A classic éclair recipe filled with vanilla custard and glazed with caramel to spark lustful feelings. Serve when you want to create a lustful environment with a lover. Makes around 12 éclairs.

MAGICAL INGREDIENTS

Vanilla—Enhances sexual desire and personal empowerment
Sugar—Enhances feelings of love
Molasses (found in brown sugar)—Compels and lures; it also helps enhance the longevity of spell work.
Eggs—Ripeness, readiness, and sexual vitality
Cream—Vitality and strength

As you handle and prepare the ingredients, infuse sexual desire, lust, and confidence into each one. It can be difficult if you're not really feeling it, but you can encourage these feelings by focusing on a moment when you felt that way. If you're not feeling sexy when you're preparing the vanilla, think of a time when you felt irresistible. Think of an event, a moment, a time, and remember how you felt, how good and wonderful it was. You can do it! When you eat the dish, you will feel those feelings again.

PÂTE À CHOUX DOUGH INGREDIENTS

- 1½ cups water
- 1 stick butter
- 2 teaspoons sugar
- 1¾ cups flour
- 9 eggs
- A heavy pinch of salt

PÂTE À CHOUX INSTRUCTIONS

1. Preheat your oven to 425° F.
2. Add water, butter, sugar, and salt to a large pot over medium-high heat.
3. Once it is boiling, add in the flour and mix until the dough forms a ball.
4. Add one egg at a time, fully incorporating each before adding the next.
5. Let your dough rest for about 30 minutes. Now would be a great time to start your custard.
6. When ready, pipe the dough onto a parchment-lined baking sheet, about 3 inches long and ½ inch wide.
7. Bake your dough for 15 minutes. Lower your oven temperature to 375° F and bake for an additional 10 minutes.
8. Let cool.

TONYA A. BROWN   FEBRUARY 2019

> Additional helpful tools:
> parchment paper, pastry bag with round tip, candy or food thermometer, and mixer

VANILLA CUSTARD INGREDIENTS

- 2 cups whole milk
- 2 teaspoons sugar
- 2 teaspoons cornstarch
- 1 vanilla pod
- 3 egg yolks + 1 whole egg
- ¼ cup butter
- A heavy pinch of salt

VANILLA CUSTARD INSTRUCTIONS

1. Add your milk and (opened and scraped) vanilla pod to a pan over medium-high heat. Once it starts to boil, remove from the burner and let sit for about 15 minutes.
2. Using a hand mixer, add sugar, salt, corn starch, butter, and eggs to a bowl and beat until pale yellow.
3. Bring your vanilla milk back onto the burner, remove the vanilla pod, and add in the beat-egg mixture. Whisk until the custard is thick and creamy. Transfer to a bowl.
4. Cover your custard with cling film directly onto the surface of the custard and let chill in the fridge for 2 hours.

INGREDIENTS FOR CARAMEL

- 1 cup white sugar
- 1 cup brown sugar
- ⅔ cup water
- ⅔ cup heavy cream

CARAMEL INSTRUCTIONS

1. In a small pot over medium-high heat, add in your water and sugars. Mix well. Let your water and sugar mixture boil until it reaches a temperature of 235° F or the "soft ball" phase.
2. Add in your heavy cream and mix well.
3. Let your caramel rest until it reaches a glazing thickness for you to dip your éclairs in.

ÉCLAIR ASSEMBLY INSTRUCTIONS

1. Using a small knife, create a crosshatch cut on both ends of your éclair shells. This will allow them to open up to the piping tip.
2. Fill your piping bag with custard and fill your dough shells with custard.
3. Dip your éclairs in the caramel.
4. Serve.

TIP

Lavender oil is known as one of the most calming of essential oils. In aromatherapy, it is used for relaxation and to relieve tension. In magic, lavender can be used for happiness, love, purification, and wisdom. Combine lavender with rose geranium oil for fulfilling love and happiness.

–Kiki Dombrowski

KITCHEN WITCH SPELLS

LUXURIOUS BODY MOISTURIZERS

YOU WILL NEED
+ Shea butter (may substitute with cocoa butter, beeswax, or coconut oil)
+ Lavender oil
+ Lime oil

※

You can make body moisturizers from so many ingredients, including beeswax, coconut oil, cocoa butter, and more, but here I'm using shea butter. Feel free to use whichever is most accessible for you.

☽

In a bowl, add 150 grams of shea butter, 10 drops of lavender oil, and up to 10 drops of lime oil.

✳

The lavender relaxes and promotes peace, and the lime gently invigorates and uplifts, the end result being that you feel calm and relaxed but also happy and inspired. Plus, the combination smells sweetly adorable, and you'll have super soft and silky skin.

EMMA KATHRYN · FEBRUARY 2019

PART IV

THE LOVERS' ROSE SALVE

YOU WILL NEED
+ 1 cup olive oil
+ 5 drops rose oil
+ 1 ounce beeswax
+ ½ teaspoon thyme
+ 1 teaspoon rosemary
+ 1 handful dried red rose petals
+ 1 handful dried pink rose petals
+ 1 teaspoon crushed rose thorns
+ 3 drops blood (from the witch and a lover)

INSTRUCTIONS
Pour 1 cup of olive oil into a glass jar. Add your herbs (rose petals, crushed thorns for penetrating/ binding hearts, rosemary and thyme). Add 5 drops of rose oil and 3 drops of blood into the herb mixture.

Allow this mixture to sit for 3 – 6 weeks so the properties of the herbs may be absorbed into the oil. After 3 – 6 weeks have passed, warm 1 ounce of beeswax on the stove on low/medium heat.

When the beeswax is melted, add your oil/herb mixture into the pot. Stir the wax and oil well.

Pour the mixture into a container (tin is recommended) and allow it to cool and harden.

A fountain of blood pours from my crown of roses.

I need to be thin so that you are able to swallow this soreness of red flowering, putridity, the chrysalis.
I worship in my wet death-gown of blushing flesh.

The crafting of magickal salves was an important tradition passed down from one Satanic witch to another within my bloodline. Most of the ointments made by myself and my witch foremothers have been crafted to be of aid during sex rituals or the performance of love magick serving to bond two hearts to each other eternally in the presence of our deliciously dark god.

USE/APPLICATION
Before using this salve, perform a spot test. Apply a pea-sized amount of the salve to the inside of your wrist to make sure you do not have an allergic reaction. Discontinue use if irritation occurs. Before a sex ritual, anoint your skin (and your lover's) with the salve, applying it to your wrists, ankles, temples, forehead, and over the heart. You may anoint your entire body if you wish but avoid sensitive areas and the mucous membranes.

KITCHEN WITCH SPELLS

ATTRACTION OIL

YOU WILL NEED
- Amber oil
- Patchouli oil
- Cinnamon oil*
- Geranium oil*
- Jasmine oil*

*optional

☽ ✳ ☾

A simple oil blend you can make to attract others to you is equal parts patchouli and amber essential oils. If you want to attract passion add a drop of cinnamon. If you want to want to attract romance and love add a drop of jasmine. If you want to attract friendship add a drop of geranium.

PART IV

STRAWBERRY AND CHOCOLATE FACE MASK

YOU WILL NEED

- Bowl
- 4 strawberries
- ½ of an avocado
- ½ teaspoon vanilla extract
- 10 drops rosehip essential oil
- 4 tablespoons of cocoa powder
- ½ tablespoon of crushed rose petals

☾

This one is a personal favorite of mine, and you'll see why. It smells good enough to eat (it is indeed edible!) and is super easy to whip up for a luxurious and decadent treat.

✶

In a bowl, using a food processor if you have one (if you don't have one, you can simply mash the ingredients together until you reach the desired consistency), add four ripe strawberries, half an avocado, four tablespoons of cocoa powder, half a tablespoon of crushed rose petals, half a teaspoon of vanilla extract, and 10 drops of rosehip essential oil.

☽

Apply evenly to your face, lay back, and relax for 10 minutes with some soothing music playing in the background. Rinse off with warm water. This one is fun to make for a girly night in with close friends over a bottle of white wine.

✶

I hope you enjoy this luxurious treat! Whether you are single, in a relationship, or anywhere in between, remember that love of self should be at the very core. We witches are worth it too!

EMMA KATHRYN — FEBRUARY 2019

KITCHEN WITCH SPELLS

LOVING HERBAL STICK

YOU WILL NEED
- Cotton string
- Scissors
- Lavender
- Yarrow
- Roses

STEP 1
Collect the herbs and flowers you wish to use. For a Loving Herbal Stick use roses, lavender, and yarrow. Only pick what you need, and do not pick anything that is rare, may have pesticides on it, or that you do not have permission to harvest.

STEP 2
Decide the size of the herbal stick you want. If you want larger herbal sticks, make sure that there is enough stem and the plants you collect are between seven and ten inches. You can also make smaller ones that are only between three and five inches.

STEP 3
Clean and arrange the plants. Make sure that all the stems are at facing downward and the flowers/tops of the plants are facing upward.

STEP 4
Gather all the ingredients together at the bottoms of the herbal stick and tie it together with a strong knot. This is the base of the herbal stick, so use a lot of string to wrap this tightly.

STEP 5
Slowly start to wrap the string from the base upward toward the tip of the herbal stick. Make sure that you wrap them tightly. When you reach the top area where you want to stop, start wrapping the string back down toward the base of the stick. When you get to the bottom tie the string off with another strong knot.

STEP 6
Hang the herbal sticks to dry. I like to hang them to air dry in front of a window. You can also dry them on a rack. It will take at least a week for the bundles to dry out completely, depending on the size of the herbal stick.

KIKI DOMBROWSKI

PART IV

TIP

Using the sugar from your kitchen cupboard, add shredded rose petals and lavender flowers and a couple of drops of rosehip oil. Use this as a gentle skin scrub, suitable for use all over your body. The gentleness of the sugar will smooth skin, and the rose and lavender will leave you feeling relaxed and calm. Rosehip oil is particularly good for skin, especially for reducing the look of skin imperfections, including scarring.

–Emma Kathryn

KITCHEN WITCH SPELLS

FACIAL TONIC FOR ATTRACTION

YOU WILL NEED
- Organic apple cider vinegar or neutral grain spirit (vodka)
- Organic rose petals
- Cheesecloth
- Spray bottle
- Mason jar
- Water
- Bowl

RECIPE
- 2 parts organic apple cider vinegar or 1 part neutral grain spirit (vodka)
- 10 parts rosewater

> Let the tried and true timelessness of roses lead you to a blissful place. Try this recipe for a rose water facial tonic.

STEP 1
Fill a bowl with organic rose petals. Pour over boiling water and let stand to cool.

Optional: Pour rose petals and water mixture into a mason jar and let sit in the sun for a day.

STEP 2
Filter petals from the water using cheesecloth; add apple cider vinegar or neutral grain spirit.

STEP 3
Store the tonic in a glass spray bottle away from heat and light, or in the door of your refrigerator.

STEP 4
Spritz onto the face after cleansing and before moisturizing morning and evening.

EM MIILLER — FEBRUARY 2016

PART IV

HOT CHOCOLATE FOR A LOVING HOME

DISH
Decadent Hot Chocolate
with Peppermint Rose Whipped Cream

INTENTION
Encourage warmth and love into a family's home

WHEN TO EAT OR SERVE
When you are spending a night in with your family

There is nothing as fitting for the holidays as a mug full of warm, creamy hot chocolate. As the temperature drops, I've found myself craving this drinkable dessert more and more. This hot chocolate recipe is meant to help bring warmth and love into the home. The experience will begin with cool rose peppermint cream before turning toward warmth with this spicy hot chocolate concoction—this is meant to by symbolic of what we're trying to bring into our lives: warmth, spice, and love. If you do not like the taste of rose or find it difficult to acquire, leaving it out will not change the magical properties of this hot chocolate recipe.

TONYA A. BROWN   DECEMBER 2018

MAGICAL INGREDIENTS

Rose—Rose is bright and brings an intense love that balances well with the intensity of the chocolate.
Peppermint—Peppermint is said to bring happiness.
Chocolate—Chocolate brings love, grounding, and prosperity.
Cinnamon—Cinnamon brings healing and warmth.
Cayenne—Cayenne is the ultimate warmth spice.
Salt—Salt is the symbol of protection.

As you handle and prepare the ingredients, infuse warmth, love, and happiness into each respective ingredient.

ROSE MINT WHIPPED CREAM INGREDIENTS

+ 1 cup heavy cream
+ 2 teaspoons powdered sugar
+ 1 teaspoon peppermint extract
+ ½ teaspoon rose water

SPICY HOT CHOCOLATE INGREDIENTS

+ 2 cups of your favorite milk (non-fat, almond, coconut, etc.)
+ ⅓ cup of your favorite chocolate (dark works well)
+ Pinch of cinnamon, cayenne, and salt to taste

RECIPE

1. In a small saucepan, add 2 cups of milk and set the heat to low.
2. While the milk starts to heat, add all of your whipped cream ingredients into a bowl. Using a hand mixer, whip them to a soft peak. Taste to determine if more sugar is needed.
3. Add chocolate, cinnamon, salt, and cayenne into your saucepan with milk and mix with a whisk or wooden spoon until smooth.
4. Remove hot chocolate from stove once the milk starts to steam. Taste to determine if more spice is needed.

PART IV

DRAW LOVE FLOOR WASH

YOU WILL NEED
- Herbs and plant matter, including essential oils
- Alcohol (a spirit with an alcohol content of at least 30%, perhaps a rum, vodka, or brandy)
- A clean glass bottle with lid or stopper
- A clean glass jar with lid

> Floor washes are an excellent way of adding a touch of magic into your everyday life, and with this one, a dash of romance too!

STEP 1

Choose four or five different herbs or plants to use in your wash. Use dry plant matter, as this will let your wash keep for longer without spoiling. There are many herbs and plants associated with love. Feel free to chop and change the ingredients depending on what you have available. Plants all have more than one quality. Consider these other associations as you decide which to add to your wash. That's the beauty of washes—you can tailor them to specifically match your intentions. It's worth mentioning that you don't need to add all of the ingredients listed, and I would actually advise against it.

HERBS FOR LOVE

Evening Primrose—desirability, love
Cardamon—love, lust, and fidelity
Rose Petals—classical, romantic love; especially pink or red roses
Ginger—sensuality, sexuality
Chamomile—relaxation, love
Chili Peppers—passion, love
Lavender—harmony, love
Poppy—love, abundance
Rosemary—love, lust
Basil—love, success
Willow—drawing and strengthening love

> If you're looking for something lusty and passionate, you might include red rose petals, chili peppers, and ginger, adding drops of rosemary oil.
> If you're after something more relaxed, a more romantic love, then lavender, chamomile, willow (leaf or bark), or pink rose petals with lavender and rosemary oil.

EMMA KATHRYN — FEBRUARY 2019

STEP 2

Take your glass jar and add all of your chosen herbs/plants/flowers. I always say don't be shy with your servings; how much you need will largely depend on the size of the jar you are using. I normally add by sight, though a good rule to follow is two parts mellow ingredients to one part stronger. So, for example, if using rose petals and chili peppers, use two parts rose petals to one part chili. Of course, you can also add more or less of one ingredient, depending on what specifically you want.

STEP 3

Now it's time to add the alcohol. Pour your chosen spirit into the jar so that all of the plant ingredients are covered. And that's it! Time to leave the ingredients to infuse for at least a week.

STEP 4

While the ingredients are infusing, it's important to add your own intent, your own will. It's time to weave your own magic! Once a day, spend some time in meditation over your jar. Focus on what you want to draw to yourself. Chant over the jar. Shake it and utter:

With this wash, I draw to me Love and lust and harmony.

Or you can write your own chant, and I urge you to give it a go. It doesn't matter if your words aren't poetic, so long as they are true! What is important is that you spend time with your mixture, infusing it with your intent, will, and desires.

STEP 4

Now it's time to strain the liquid. Use a sieve or a muslin cloth to drain the liquid, squeezing as much as you can from the plant matter. Funnel the liquid into a clean jar or bottle and add any essential oils. Secure the lid, and your wash is ready!

STEP 5

To use your wash, add it by the capful to your bucket, along with your regular detergent. Add it to the sink to clean worktops. Use it on a cloth to clean surfaces such as window sills, doors, and even in the bathroom. I use mine everywhere! Get a spray bottle, dilute a couple of capfuls with water, and spray into the air. As you wash and clean, utter your chant or spell. Focus on what you are aiming to achieve. Play some meditation music and let the act of cleaning be the meditation itself, all the while focusing on drawing love into your life.

PART IV

MEAL TO HELP MEND STRAINED RELATIONSHIPS

When fall comes and moves us into the darker side of the year, we retreat into our homes to create warmth and happiness. Often this time of year is when we interact with those in our lives who we may not have the best relationship with. This pizza helps new and old friends find a happier relationship.

As you handle and prepare the ingredients, infuse the feelings of a new journey, turning negative feelings into positive ones, and higher vibrations into them. This can be difficult if you're not really feeling it, but you can fake it if need be. If you're feeling depressed and you're preparing the basil, you need to feel positive. Think of a time when you felt really joyous and happy. Think of an event, a moment, a time, and remember how you felt, how good and wonderful it was. You can do it! When you eat the dish, you will feel those feelings again.

MAGICAL INGREDIENTS

Meat—Enhances the power of the other ingredients
Basil—Turns negative feelings into positive feelings
Mushrooms—Open up new gateways
Tomatoes—Keep away negativity
Cheese—Raises vibrations

> If you want to make the meal vegetarian, removing the meat will not damage the recipe

INGREDIENTS

- Frozen or handmade dough
- 1 cup tomato sauce
- 1 cup shredded mozzarella
- ¼ lb cooked ground sausage
- 4 ounces sliced mushrooms
- 4 ounces mozzarella balls
- 1 bunch fresh basil
- 2 tablespoons pesto (optional)

INSTRUCTIONS

1. Preheat oven to 500° F with an upside down baking sheet heating in the oven.
2. Flour a cutting board surface and then roll your dough to desired shape and consistency.
3. Work fast to layer pizza with sauce, shredded cheese, mushrooms, sausage, and mozzarella balls.
4. Using the cutting board slide the pizza on top of the hot baking sheet within the oven.
5. Bake for 10-15 minutes.
6. Once finished remove from oven and add basil leaves and pesto.

PART IV

COOKING MAGIC FOR LOVE

Cooking can be a loving magic all on it's own. When cooking for a partner on date night there are a few different ways you can add energetic passion and love into the food. On the next page you will find examples of various ingredients and their uses. Use these items in the kitchen when creating date night meals or any time you would like to encourage passion and love.

ANDREA MALDONADO — ADAPTED FROM JULY 2016

KITCHEN WITCH SPELLS

LOVE — Oranges
Cumin
Cloves

PASSION — Alcoholic Spirits
Strawberries
Coffee

EMPOWERMENT — Allspice
Paprika
Tomatoes (Sundried Too)

PURIFICATION — Bay Leaves
Lemons

DOMINATION — Limes
Hot Peppers

FERTILITY — Garlic
Pomegranate

LUST — Cinnamon
Cardamom
Honey

PART V
DEITY WORK

PART V

GUIDED TOWARD LOVE
WORKING LOVE MAGIC WITH DEITIES

Love is a highly complex emotion, and you are doing yourself a disservice if you only have deities add a bit of power to your spells. They can help your spell work, of course, but unless you are in a place in your life that is accommodating to love, the relationship (be it professional, platonic, or romantic) will not last. If you establish a bond with one or more gods, those deities can guide you toward love by aiding you in aspects of your life that play direct and indirect roles in your relationships. Deities can aid you in trust, self-acceptance, in accepting that it's OK to be alone, and, most importantly, teach you about happiness.

Trust is probably one of the most important things in a relationship, as trust is the glue that binds us together, be it a kinship, friendship, or romantic partnership. Establishing trust in deities helped me learn to trust in people and has greatly impacted the love I have for people in my life. For the gods to help you learn trust, however, you must first figure out, through meditation and/or divination, why you can't trust. Ask deities to help you figure out the why, and together you can figure out the how. It may be as simple as deities keeping their promises to you to show you trust is possible, or it may be a year long journey, but either way it's worth the effort. Trust is soothing to the soul, settling to the mind, and balm to an aching heart.

If I've learned anything about gods, it's that they don't give a shit about what people think of them and this attitude can easily be blessed unto people they work with. For me, working with The Morrigan helped me gain confidence, which allowed me to maintain pride even when others put me down. This, combined with the realization that other people's opinion of me is actually none of my business, has helped me make much wiser choices when it comes to love and relationships. More importantly, it has instilled in me the courage to accept myself and my actions. Love is doomed if we do not accept our own sexuality – our sexual activity and our sexual preference. Now that I accept who I am wholly, I can have that fling, I can have that relationship, and I can be happy with myself and my choices.

Ironically, finding happiness in being alone has helped my love life the most. Maintaining dignity, pride, and confidence in being single instilled in me the patience and wisdom necessary to choose a partner that was going to compliment my life. With the strength to be alone, and not lonely, I found happiness. And it was in accepting that I could be alone that I learned probably the most important lesson about relationships: happiness must come from within. It's not your partner's job to 'make' you happy and putting such a responsibility on someone else is unfair. It will lead to resentment, and eventually end the relationship. Deities can certainly help you, firstly, figure out what you need to be happy, and then how to obtain it.

Love can come into your life, but if you're not in a position to accept and give love in a healthy manner, it won't stay. So, before asking deities to aid you in your love spells, perhaps you may ask them to help you with things that have pushed love out of your life. The examples above are based on my personal experiences, but know this: if devotional practices with deities can help me, they can help you, no matter the problem.

–Amanda Wilson, *Writer*

On New Year's Eve there is a belief that you should kiss the person you want to keep kissing in the new year. In Denmark there is a tradition of throwing plates at doors to banish bad luck. So, if you throw a plate at the door of a friend it is meant to symbolize friendship. If you don't feel like chucking plate ware at your pal's house, consider a little more

...

PRIVATE TRADITION THAT IS CELEBRATED IN MEXICO AND BRAZIL. IN THESE NATIONS THERE IS A BELIEF THAT CERTAIN COLORED UNDERGARMENTS ON NEW YEAR'S EVE CAN INFLUENCE THE KIND OF YEAR YOU WILL HAVE. IF YOU WEAR NEW RED UNDERWEAR YOU WILL HAVE A YEAR OF ROMANCE. OR, SHARE FOOD GIFTS MADE WITH APPLES OR CHOCOLATE WITH THOSE YOU LOVE, AS THEY ARE BOTH FOODS OF LOVE.

– KIKI DOMBROWSKI

PART V

> **TIP**
>
> To add a punch to any lust/sex charms add dried olive leaves.
>
> —Michelle Denison

DEITY WORK

HONOURING JUNO

Honoring Juno is honoring all women, all mothers, all, wives, and all children. To honor Juno, plant a lily and watch it begin to bloom in June. Send her, and the women in your life appreciation for all of the love and support that they give you, and honor yourself as a woman by giving gratitude to yourself for all of the strength you have.

EM MIILLER   JUNE 2017

PART V

BEAUTY

Freyja's beauty was known by all. She was the inspiration of love songs and poetry. Ask for Freyja to help you with self-love, confidence, and a sense of self-worth. Laurie Sue Brockway's *A Goddess is a Girl's Best Friend* offers a wonderful exercise for creating a set of Freyja's Runes; a set of stones with sensual adjectives on them. As a spin on this idea, get a set of index cards (one to three dozen). On each index card write a word that will inspire you to feel beautiful, empowered, and confident (e.g. intriguing, mysterious, successful, prosperous, beautiful, magnetic, confident). You can decorate the cards if you are crafty. Every morning, pull a card to focus on that day. Keep the card with you and look at it frequently, knowing that you are what is stated on the card (and more). You can also wear a Freyja-inspired oil. Combine equal parts sandalwood, rose, and amber oils with a carrier oil; I recommend 13 drops of each oil, blending them together on a Friday. Put a piece of rose quartz and/or citrine in a vial with the oil.

DEITY WORK

FERTILITY

People may have prayed to Freyja to help them to bear children and to assist with fertility. If you are looking to bring children into your life, honor Freyja in your homestead. You can make a little fertility bag to keep by your bedside or under your bed. Create this during your ovulation or a new moon. Get a small green bag and draw the Berkana (B) rune on it. Fill with apple seeds, flax seeds, rose petals, hazelnuts, patchouli, and yarrow. Add carnelian, rose quartz, moonstone, and malachite crystals.

PART V

> **TIP**
>
> Blend two parts patchouli oil with one part cinnamon oil for a powerful attraction blend (keep in mind cinnamon essential oil can be an irritant, so use carefully).
>
> –Kiki Dombrowski

DEITY WORK

ATTRACTING ROMANCE

Freyja can be called upon if you are trying to bring love into your life. There are many ways to speak with Freyja about doing this. You can keep a statue of her (or a framed illustration of her) on your altar. Dress your altar with fresh flowers, such as roses or daisies. Decorate with golden objects or jewelry that you love. Light red candles near your altar, and write a letter to Freyja, telling her in detail the traits you are looking for in your mate. Explain to her why you need romance in your life, and take a moment to describe how it would feel to have that special someone arrive soon. Anoint the letter with amber essential oil, and leave it on the altar. Keep the letter with you if you'd like, or keep it with Freyja's image.

PART V

> **TIP**
>
> Amber is such an exotic, sensual fragrance that I favor above many others. It is used for love, sensuality, spiritual awareness, and attraction. Blend equal parts amber with patchouli to create an inviting fragrance.
>
> –Kiki Dombrowski

DEITY WORK

❦ LOVE ALTAR ❦

Bring love in. A "Love Altar" could be beneficial when you are trying to bring someone into your life. Adorn it with rose petals, and reminders of love that is personal to you. Walks in nature to cleanse and realign with your love-needs is a great way to gain a little love in your life. And, don't be shy to ask for help. Fairies love love too! I'm sure they would come up with an interesting mate for you! Visualize with unwavering belief, and knowledge that you deserve (hence self-love) what you want, and you will receive it.

REBECCA FERREIRA TROY   ❧   OCTOBER 2017

PART V

TIP

Ylang-Ylang: Ylang-ylang oil can be used to relieve nervousness, ease sadness, and bring a peaceful feeling into the home. In magic, it can be used for love, sensuality, and increasing desire. Blend with orange essential oil to attract new and joyous love in your life.

—Kiki Dombrowski

DEITY WORK

CELEBRATE LOVE

The Ancient Romans named the month of the summer solstice after Juno, the goddess of marriage and childbirth. June has long been a favored month for brides who have used the fine weather for the perfect outdoor wedding. Make the day an opportunity to spend with your romantic partner. You can take time on summer solstice showing appreciation for your family, friends, and loved ones with gifts, compliments, and affection. And most importantly, show love toward yourself. Treat yourself to a special day: get a massage, go shopping, or take a nap to relax. If you would like to try a more traditional practice of self-love, collect dew on the morning of the summer solstice. It is said that washing with the dew will create youthful beauty.

KIKI DOMBROWSKI — JUNE 2016

CONCLUSION
THE POWER OF LOVE

So there you have it, a book brimming with the power of love! And no doubt, as you've worked your way through, you will have noticed there are so many different types of love and even more ways you can bring them into your life. Part of why I love being a part of the *Witch Way* family is because of the sheer diversity of not only the writers but also of you, the readers, and I think this is what makes this little book of love all the more important, because love is one of those universal and unifying forces of which there can never be enough in the world. All of the things that separate us pale into insignificance when compared with the power of love.

Within these pages, you have encountered many spells, workings, and rituals that all aim to bring love in all of its forms into your life. I am of the firm belief that as witches, as magical beings, we are each more than capable of deciding what we are comfortable doing and what we are not. We each have our own moral compasses that help us navigate our way through this life, along our own unique crooked paths.

Whether we want more romantic love, passion, familial love, friendly love, or even just a little help loving ourselves more, we can use the power of magic to attract these things into our lives. By the time most of us have decided to use magic, we will have already made our minds up about what it is we want to achieve and what we are willing to do to get it. Ultimately, all magic, including love magic involves bringing about change and so as we approach love magic, it is important we do so with trust in ourselves, patience and goodwill toward others and ourselves, and above all, authenticity. All of these are needed if we wish to manifest our wants, dreams, and desires into reality.

Love magic requires the patience to decide what it is we really want and need, not to rush ourselves or others, goodwill in our workings and a faith that they will work, and authenticity in actions and feelings. It is these qualities that will make the love we seek strong, true, and enduring. Love is all of these things, no matter the form it may take. All of the workings, spells, and rituals in this book embody those traits and honour love in all of its gloriously beautiful forms.

Love is what makes us strong. Love is what overcomes obstacles. Love is enduring. Love is beautiful. Quite simply, love is magic! And with that, dear readers, you find yourself at the end of this little book of love and before you set off on your own love filled adventures, I send with you this small blessing:

May your days be filled with magic and love,
Gentle and soft like the breast of a dove.
May your life be filled with all that you seek,
Beauty and love for the strong and the meek.
May the love of friendship and magic flow to you from me,
As we will it, so shall it be!

–Emma Kathryn, *Writer*

CONTRIBUTORS

TIANNA SICILIA

Tianna Sicilia lives in Southern California where she works as a writer and content strategist. In her spare time, she acts in indie films, watches too much TV, and is the co-founder of *The Witchy Podcast*, and *The Christian and the Witch,* and the founder of *The Astrology Witch Podcast*. She is also the founder of the natural beauty and lifestyle blog Storybook Apothecary.

✳

www.anchor.fm/astrologywitchpodcast

PARIS AJANA

Paris Ajana, the founder of Hoodoo Goddess LLC, is a descendant Hoodoo Candlemaker and Spiritual Advisor. Gifted with a deeper understanding, she knows firsthand how to become aligned with the process of manifestation. By utilizing spiritual and magical candles and other metaphysical tools, she works directly with individuals who are on their magical and spiritual journey. Advising based on each need, the Hoodoo Goddess guides the candle ritual choice which will aid the seeker's growth and most importantly bring spiritual transformation into their daily lives.

✳

www.hoodoogoddess.com

EMME DICE

Emme is a non-Wiccan witch living in urban Minnesota. Her curiosity of and education in cultural history compels her to collect ancient as well as modern esoteric knowledge. The nurturing of her soul, mind, and spirit through meditation is fueled by Emme's passionate belief in the power of intention. Emme also enjoys caring for her plants and two cats.

DAINA RENTON

Daina is an eclectic divination witch from Scotland. A hopeless romantic with eight cats and an unchallenged love for fog. Dark fashion photographer and tarot reader.

✳

www.dainarenton.co.uk

ANDREA MALDONADO

Andrea is an author, a graduate of the Culinary Institute of America and a High Priestess of Deam Lux. As a Witch and Chef, she creates food magic using seasonal ingredients coupled with their magical properties to amplify spells, celebrate everyday life and the wheel of the year.

✳

www.GourmetWitch.org

REBECCA FERREIRA TROY

Rebecca Ferreira Troy began reading Tarot and every Magical book she could get her hands on from 11 years old onwards. A reluctant empath and intuitive, she found her voice not through communicating with her voice, as most do, but through the written word. Her new book, *Healing and Witchcraft in a Conformist World* can be found on Amazon worldwide. Rebecca is the founder of the Unicorn School of Light.

✳

www.theunicornschooloflight.com

AMANDA WILSON

Amanda Wilson is a mother, witch, artist and writer. She loves working magic with her son, Josh, and experimenting with new ways to incorporate magic in everyday life. To learn more, check out her Author Blog.

✳

www.WriteKindofMagic.com

EMMA KATHRYN

Emma Kathryn practises traditional British Witchcraft, Obeah and Vodoun. She lives in a small rural town in the middle of England where she drinks copious amounts of coffee, reads tarot, casts spells and weaves magick!

✳

Instagram @emmakathrynwildwitch

MICHAEL HERKES

Michael Herkes (Chicago), also known as "The Glam Witch," has been practicing modern witchcraft for over 20 years. He is a devotee to the goddess Lilith and focuses his practice on crystal, glamour, love, moon, and sex magic. He is also an experienced tarot reader, nationwide speaker, contributor to *Witch Way Magazine*, and author of several books including *The GLAM Witch*.

www.theglamwitch.com

MARY ELISABETH YOUNG

Mary lives in Tampa, FL with her loving partner of eight years and their four cats.

SCARLET RAVENSWOOD

Scarlet Ravenswood is a Youtuber and writer creating content about modern paganism and witchcraft. She is dedicated to researching and providing educational material about ancient pagan traditions and folklore. She has built up an online community of over 100K and hopes to eventually create an academy and workshop where students can come to learn traditional skills such as herbalism, divination, and ritual practice.

JESSICA RIPLEY

Jessica Ripley is a Hekatean witch, writer, and spiritual advisor from Minnesota with a lifetime of study and experience in witchcraft and spiritual practice. She owns Owl in the Oak Tarot and also writes for *Patheos Pagan* under the blog "Night Owl Meditations."

✴

www.owlintheoaktarot.com

JENNY PARTEN

I am a yoga instructor, holistic practitioner/teacher, writer and public speaker. As a holistic practitioner, I am certified in many different modalities such as Acutonics Level II & I am a Reiki Master. I am a student/teacher of shamanic practices and most of my work revolves around vibratory healing. I teach traditional forms of yoga, as well as Kundalini and Buti yoga.

✴

www.jennyparten.com.

NESSA SKINNER

Nessa Skinner is an Eclectic Witch in Southern California. Some of her practices include divination, dream interpretations, spell crafting, crystals, herbs, & essential oils. She loves to craft personal gifts for her friends and family. Some of my favorite types of spell work are love, protection, and cleansings.

EFFY WINTER

Effy Winter is a writer and herbalist from Philadelphia, Pennsylvania. She is the author of *Flowers of the Flesh* (2019) and *SYLVIA* (2021). Effy currently works for *Witch Way Magazine* and resides in Kansas City, Missouri, where she manages Rose & Yew Apothecary.

https://effywinter.com

NATALIE WILSON

Natalie is an Illinois based natural herbal witch. Passionate about the earth, plants, and herbals - soaps, lotions, oils and natural perfumes became her profession. Making herbal skincare for about 20 years, her shops are full of items from soaps and bath bombs to spell oils charmed with intent, to bulk herbs and essential oil blends.

www.etsy.com/shop/naturescomfortherbs
www.etsy.com/shop/thistleandroseshop

MICHELLE DENISON

Michelle is a kitchen witch and herbalist living in Southern California. Her mission is to spread herbal awareness and education as far and wide as possible.

Instagram @glitterinthedirt
www.thetwigandfeather.com

KIKI DOMBROWSKI

Kiki is a spiritual researcher and explorer who has spent her life studying mythology, magic, witchcraft, and the supernatural. She lives in Savannah where she is a professional tarot card reader, certified life coach, and writer. Kiki has been a contributing writer for *Witch Way Magazine* for over five years. She self-published two books, *Eight Extraordinary Days* and *A Curious Future* – second editions will be published in 2021 with Witch Way. She has contributed writing to the *Wicca Book of Spells Witches' Planner 2021*. She has been on many podcasts including *The Witch Daily Show*, *Some Other Sphere Podcast*, and *The Conspirinormal Podcast*.

✳

Instagram @Kikiscauldron

EM MIILLER

Em is the Owner of Isola Herbals: a company that creates non-toxic, all-natural, herbal-infused skincare and haircare remedies, and offers Herbalism and Iridology consults. She grows her own medicinal herbs in the beautiful prairies of Alberta, Canada. Em's passion for a lifestyle that embraces nature led her to pursue education in Herbalism, Traditional Chinese Medicine, and Ayurvedic Medicine. She is working towards her Clinical Herbalism certification. As an Iridologist, Em directs her attention towards equine iridology - reading the eyes of horses! Em holds a full-time career as a wine and spirits expert. She spends freetime being active outdoors with her horses Gatzby and Tobi, kitties and her Jack Russell puppy, Chloé, and practices classical ballet.

CONTRIBUTORS

EDITOR

TONYA A. BROWN

Tonya A. Brown is a current resident of New Orleans, Louisiana, where she is the editor in chief of *Witch Way Magazine* as well as writer and host of the podcast *The Witch Daily Show*. Tonya is a Lenormand reader, medium, and magical guide for other witches.

www.ingramcontent.com/pod-product-compliance
Lightning Source LLC
Chambersburg PA
CBHW070425010526
44118CB00014B/1907